LUDHAM

A NORFOLK VILLAGE

1800 - 1900

Published in 1999 by:-

E. Mumby
Willow Cottage
Decoy Road
Potter Heigham
Norfolk
NR29 5LX

ISBN 0 9535293 0 4

Produced by The University of East Anglia Print Group

LUDHAM

A NORFOLK VILLAGE

1800 - 1900

JOAN M. SNELLING

Location of Ludham, Norfolk

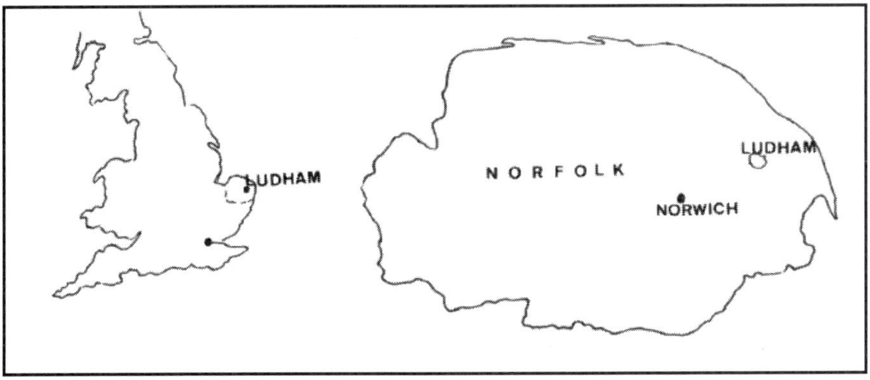

Note: *I am unable to give reference numbers of Ludham Documents now in the Norfolk Record Office, as they were deposited there after I left.*

Plate 1. (Cover)

This painting by C. H. Harrison 1842-1902 of Ludham Dyke shows the Old Staithe with two wherries moored beside the Staithe House. Next to the house is a lime kiln and storage sheds for merchandise for river transport.

Reproduced by kind permission of Geoffrey Allan of Mandell's Gallery, Elm Hill, Norwich, in whose catalogue it appeared about thirty years ago. Present owner unknown.

Contents

Page No.

List of Plates

Page No.

List of Plates continued

Page No.

List of Maps and Figures

Page No.

Introduction

This book is an account of Ludham during the nineteenth century. It is based on the original contents of the Ludham church chest, which have since all been deposited in the Norfolk Record Office. The chest was full to the top of mostly nineteenth century documents and papers and the church registers from 1583 onwards. All these I read, sorted and catalogued when I was one of Ludham's churchwardens and a member of the Bishop's Committee for Books and Documents.

The book also owes something to my personal knowledge of the parish landscape. Ever since I first pedalled around the lanes as a twelve year old, I have been looking and wondering. I also had the great good luck to have been a farm labourer during the war, at a time when farming was much the same as it had been during the previous century and earlier. Like most of the earlier inhabitants of Ludham of that time, I knew what it was like to spread muck with a fork all day, to stand shoves of corn so that the breeze will blow through them, to load a cart, to plough and to harrow and to lead a horse hoeing all day. I also learnt that biblical gesture of 'broadcasting', though it was fertiliser and not seed, and I once measured a marsh with a chain, just like the enclosure commissioners must have done 140 years before me.....

I owe a great debt to the tutors of the University of Cambridge Board of Extra-Mural Studies. The first local history course that I attended was by Rachel Young in 1956 and it was a revelation to me. Suddenly everything began to fall into place and make sense. The course was at Potter Heigham School, as Ludham didn't have a Workers' Educational Association in those days and Rachel was so kind and took such trouble to answer our questions.

Many other courses followed that one; I often went to Madingley Hall when Lionel Munby was tutor, and heard such speakers as Professor Darby on Domesday Book and George Ewart-Evans on the Oral Tradition. There too I learned palaeography from the late F. G. Emmison. Over the years there were many other courses with Chris Barringer and David Dymond, and numerous archaeological training digs with John Alexander. To all these people, I owe my thanks for their kindness, patience and unflagging enthusiasm.

Then there was Peter Boardman, in whose ancient Hornet Moth we flew from the old wartime airfield, whose runway was littered with straw bales and coils of wire, to look at the parish from above and take photographs.

I write this at some distance in time and space from Ludham; twenty-three years and nearly a thousand miles, so letters go back and forth to my old friend, Beulah Gowing, who knows more about Ludham than anyone, and she checks a tombstone inscription for me, or the bonding of brickwork on a wall ...

Then there are the descendants of old Ludham families, like Chesney England of the millwright family, Raymond Page and John Garrett, who have all sent me useful information, as have Bill and Kathleen Sloper of the Methodist Church. Sadly, the people who remembered their young days in the village for me have all passed on; Arthur Newton, Clifford Kittle and Margaret Keeler.

Last, but far from least, I am so grateful to Berry Ritchie, Trisha Drake and my daughter Elaine Mumby for their help in producing this book and to the Ludham Parish Council for so generously giving a 'Millenium Fund' grant to assist with the printing.

Thank you, everyone, and please excuse my errors and omissions.

Joan M. Snelling 1999

La Tour sur Orb, France

A Look at the Parish in 1800

Ludham is situated in Norfolk near the coast, about twenty feet above sea level with a very fertile soil. The parish is bordered with rivers and marshland on three sides and there were four stretches of open water, of which only Cromes Broad and Womack Water survive today. These were all originally flooded peat diggings, and turf for fuel continued to be dug throughout most of the nineteenth century at Turf Fen, the Hulver and Reedham marsh.

The village is in the centre of the parish and has a very wide main street and open space at Stocks Hill, where the annual market, fair and hiring fair took place. Just to the north-west is a fresh water spring, known in the past by its Saxon name of the Pulk.

The parish in 1800 was made up of about twenty farms, of which some were farmed by their owners and some by tenants. The Bishop of Norwich was, and still is, lord of the manor, and his country house at Ludham Hall with almost 600 acres was the largest farm, and this was let to tenant farmers since the late seventeenth century. The other farms varied in size down to smallholdings of a few acres. Everything in the parish depended upon the prosperity of agriculture, which was still changing in 1800 from medieval subsistence farming into a fully commercialised activity. The previous century had brought new methods and new implements needed for the increase in productivity that was to feed the growing population.

In Ludham the old open fields were being gradually enclosed by individuals. In May 1802, the map for the parliamentary enclosure showed that the open fields were already divided into numerous small fields, though it is doubtful if many of these were either hedged or ditched to begin with. After the official enclosure, all the new allocations of land had to be planted with hawthorn hedges and ditched where necessary. In 1800 the common and other marginal lands were still open and in use, by ancient custom, for casual grazing, wood gathering and peat cutting.

The Poors' Lands, which had been left to the parish in several seventeenth century wills, were still the original pieces of land, (see Figure 9), but these were to be exchanged in two years time

Figure 1. Sketch Map of Ludham Parish in 1800.

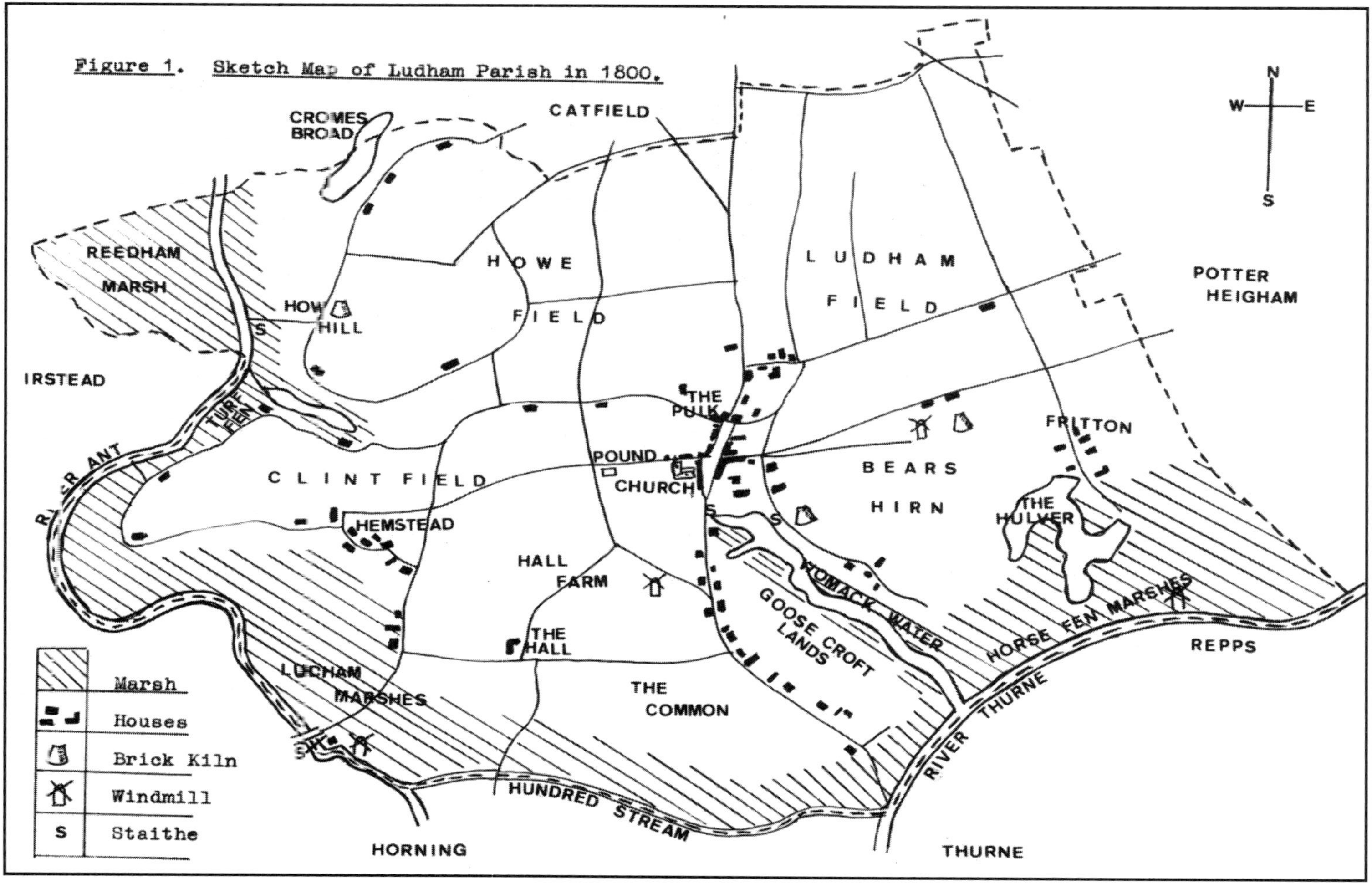

during the enclosure for marshland, some of which was used for cutting peat for fuel. Old baulks of peat-diggings were still visible from the air in the 1960s on Great Reedham marsh.

There was a large upland common of more than 80 acres in the south part of the parish, and a smaller rough bit of common at Bluebell Hole in the west.

Womack water was larger, with far more acres of open water, but the new cut had not yet been made which would make the island lower down. All the staithes were busy with river-borne trade, on Womack, where there were two staithes, and on the River Ant at How Hill and at the bridge. This bridge in 1800 was still the old medieval low arched bridge and it was to last for just over another hundred years.

Two corn mills were kept busy; the post mill in Love Lane, known as the Town Mill was turning, and so was the new tower mill up on the Yarmouth Road hill, called Ludham Mill. This was newly built by William England to replace an earlier post mill. Twenty-five years later, the tall brick windmill at How Hill would be built. Two drainage mills were in action; Horse Fen mill on the Thurne in the south-east corner of the parish, where a ferry crossed the river to Repps, and a mill just south of the bridge on the Ant. The England family were already well established as millwrights in Ludham.

At different times there have been three brick kilns in Ludham, for all local building was of brick and the soil was excellent for brick-making.

Where Horse Fen Road joins the Yarmouth Road was known as the Pit corner, because of a large pond where horses drank. This was there until the 1930s. There must have been at least three hundred horses in 1800, for work and for transport, keeping the blacksmiths and harness maker busy. The roads were just dirt tracks, some wider than others, all full of cart ruts and muddy in the wet weather. In spite of this, people still got about and the carriers' carts were continually active, carrying both goods and people. Repairing the roads was the responsibility of the parish surveyor of highways. He had to obtain the necessary loads of sand and gravel and was in charge during the regular road-mending weeks, when everyone had to help.

This was to be the last century of the parish officers, but in 1800 they were still being elected each year at the vestry meeting of ratepayers. Some tried to avoid being elected as it could be a great burden and there could be trouble if one didn't do the job properly. Besides the surveyor of highways there was the parish constable. If a man did not want to become constable, he could pay a substitute to do it for him, but this could be expensive. His job was to keep order and to enforce the law, to round up vagrants and to keep arrested persons in safe custody. He also had charge of the parish bull!

The churchwardens were, and still are, the chief officers of the parish priest. One could not legally refuse to be elected churchwarden and there was a fine of £10 if this happened. The churchwardens were helped by the beadle to keep order in church, the congregations being so much larger in those days. The pinder's task was to round up stray cattle and put them into the pound until claimed against a fine. The pound in 1800 stood halfway up the Norwich Road, at the crossroads with Love Lane and Pound Lane.

The overseers of the poor, who probably had the worst job, were responsible for relief to the poor. The poor had a very thin time indeed; each parish would only look after its own poor who had to prove their right to settle there before they could claim relief, which came from a poor rate decided at the vestry meeting. They were harried around from one place to another, sometimes a very long way. It was said, that if a body was found drowned in the river, that it would be put hastily onto the opposite bank, so as not to be chargeable to the parish!

In 1800 the splendid church of St. Catherine was the centre of worship for the population, although some were starting to break away to form a group of Wesleyan Methodists who met for worship in a private house until their first chapel could be built, twenty-one years later. The Baptists were also beginning to form a small congregation apart. John Oldershaw was the vicar of Ludham from 1795 to 1833. He was also vicar of Ranworth with Upton, and perhaps it was there that he lived, as there was no vicarage in Ludham at that time and it was not until about 1824 that a house in Staithe Road came to be used as a vicarage. The vicar's income came largely from the eighteen acres of glebe land, which made up the parson's farm and from some of the tithes collected. Tithe was a tenth part of the produce of the land; great tithes being corn, hay and wool and small tithes almost anything else, such as eggs, hens, potatoes or fruit.

The population in 1800 was 724 people; 352 males and 372 females. Of these, 56 were farm workers and 72 were in trade. They consisted of 151 families who lived in 114 houses of which 2 were empty. This seems to leave 37 families without a home, but the likely explanation is that a house or cottage was usually a building divided into two or three tenements. Housing conditions for the poorer people were dreadful; often only one bedroom for several children and their parents, a smoky, sometimes damp living room with a lean-to scullery behind, a shared privy outside and one well for several dwellings. This was in the middle of the Napoleonic wars with France and times were very hard. A lack of continental supplies caused a shortage of grain and bread prices had recently doubled.

At this time it was still the custom for many farm workers to 'live-in' on the farm. These were known as farm 'servants'. They were hired by the year - the hiring fair at Ludham continued until mid-century - and though their wages were small, they were fed and lodged and had a certain security. Because of the rising price of corn, farmers had begun to enlarge their acreage of cereals, which being less labour intensive, caused unemployment. Thus it became more economic to hire farm labourers by the day or week for a cash wage and give up the old custom. By mid-century there would be only ten farm servants living-in on Ludham farms.

The farms were almost the same as those which survive today, although now some are only dwelling houses and the land is farmed by someone else. Three had not yet been built in 1800; The Grange, which was to replace the older Malthouse Farm in 1839, Coldharbour Farm and High House Farm. The huge, beautiful barn next to the last-named was already there, long before the house. Sadly, it has now gone. (See Plate 10)

Many other fine barns, which still stand in Ludham, were very much in use in 1800 for storing corn and for threshing with flails in the old way. Most of these barns date from the previous century and have their date on the gable ends. An earlier one is at the Hall Farm, built in 1627 and a smaller but identical one at Pages Farm, presumably of the same date.

Plate 2. Church Street (The Norwich Road). Photograph, the author

The population was concentrated mainly in Ludham village in the centre of the parish, but there were two outlying hamlets, which had grown up on each side as prosperity increased.

On the west was Hempstead or Hemstead hamlet, situated along the lane running from Whitegate Farm (The Limes) to White House Farm (now demolished). There were about twenty or more dwellings along this lane, which was called Clint Street; today there is one cottage. On the east side Fritton hamlet still exists, but there were a lot more dwellings there in 1800. From Staithe

Road down to Coldharbour was then fairly well populated; there were a few houses around How Hill and down Horse Fen Road. Johnson Street, which was then called Wood Street, had a little cluster, including the Dog Inn, but that must have been an older house, as the present one looks too modern. From an entry in the church register of the burial of 'Mary Thaxter from the Dog-house' in 1689, we know there must have been an earlier house there.

Plate 3. The Yarmouth Road. Photograph, the author

Other public houses in 1800 were the Rose and Crown, (now Crown House) the Royal Exchange, (now Sunnyside) and the Kings Arms. The Bakers Arms was not yet known by that name; it was a retail beer house with communal bake-offices at the rear. The name came later. There was another bake-house just down Staithe Road. (See Plate 49) In those days people took their bread and pies to cook in the communal ovens, as they only had an open hearth at home. In the enclosure claims papers of 1801 a certain John Patterson claimed 'a public house called The Ship, with outhouses and 3 roods of land in Ludham'. It is thought that this was the larger house in the centre of the thatched row of houses on the Yarmouth Road. (See Plate 3).

There were several shops in the village and much industry; millwrights, wheelwrights, carpenters, saddler, blacksmiths, tailors, shoemakers, bricklayers, dressmakers and so on.

It was a close knit busy community in Ludham in 1800. The prosperity of each depended upon the others and all depended upon agriculture. Any changes in the fortunes of farming were usually reflected by changes in the rural society.

Most of the subjects in this section will be dealt with more fully in the rest of this book.

Sources:
Faden's map of 1797
Enclosure map of Ludham in May, 1802
Map of East Norfolk, 1827

Plate 4. The medieval bridge and the little flint and thatch cottage known as Bridge House. The steam pumphouse in the centre was not there in 1800. Old postcard.

1800 - 1802, The Enclosure in Ludham

One of the first events that happened in Ludham in the nineteenth century was the enclosure and among the parish documents in the chest were the map, an extract from the award and a paper to the vicar, setting out his glebe allotments, for the land that he farmed.

Since early medieval times many English villages had three or more open fields, divided up into long narrow 'strips' of land. Each man had several strips in each field and there he grew what he needed for his family; wheat for bread, barley for beer and oats and pulses for his few animals. He also needed to graze his animals and for this he had certain rights on the common and wasteland. The lord of the manor had his own estate apart, as in this case, the Bishop of Norwich at Ludham Hall.

This open field farming was not very efficient and men began gradually to enclose blocks of strips with fences, having obtained the strips from their neighbours, either by agreement or threat, thus making small fields or closes. Enclosure was a continuous process, going on at varying degrees since medieval times. It caused controversy everywhere; Kett's rebellion in 1549 at Wymondham was caused by disputes over enclosure fences. Many complaints were concerned with the ending of the open fields and the commons. Ludham had three large open fields and a smaller one. Their names are found in lists of glebe and town lands; How Field, Ludham North Field, (or just Ludham Field) Bears Hirn and Clint Field. The common was on the southern upland of the parish, overlooking St. Benets marshes. We know that 86 acres or so by Hall Common were definitely common, but Faden's map of 1797 puts 'dry common' right across from the Dog Inn to Coldharbour and this whole area was indeed divided up at the enclosure. (See Figure 2)

Almost all the allotments of arable land in Ludham were made in the open fields and the rest was marshland pasture. There was a lot of marshland, almost three-quarters of the parish boundary being rivers edged with marshes. From the Ludham enclosure map it can be seen that the open fields had already been enclosed

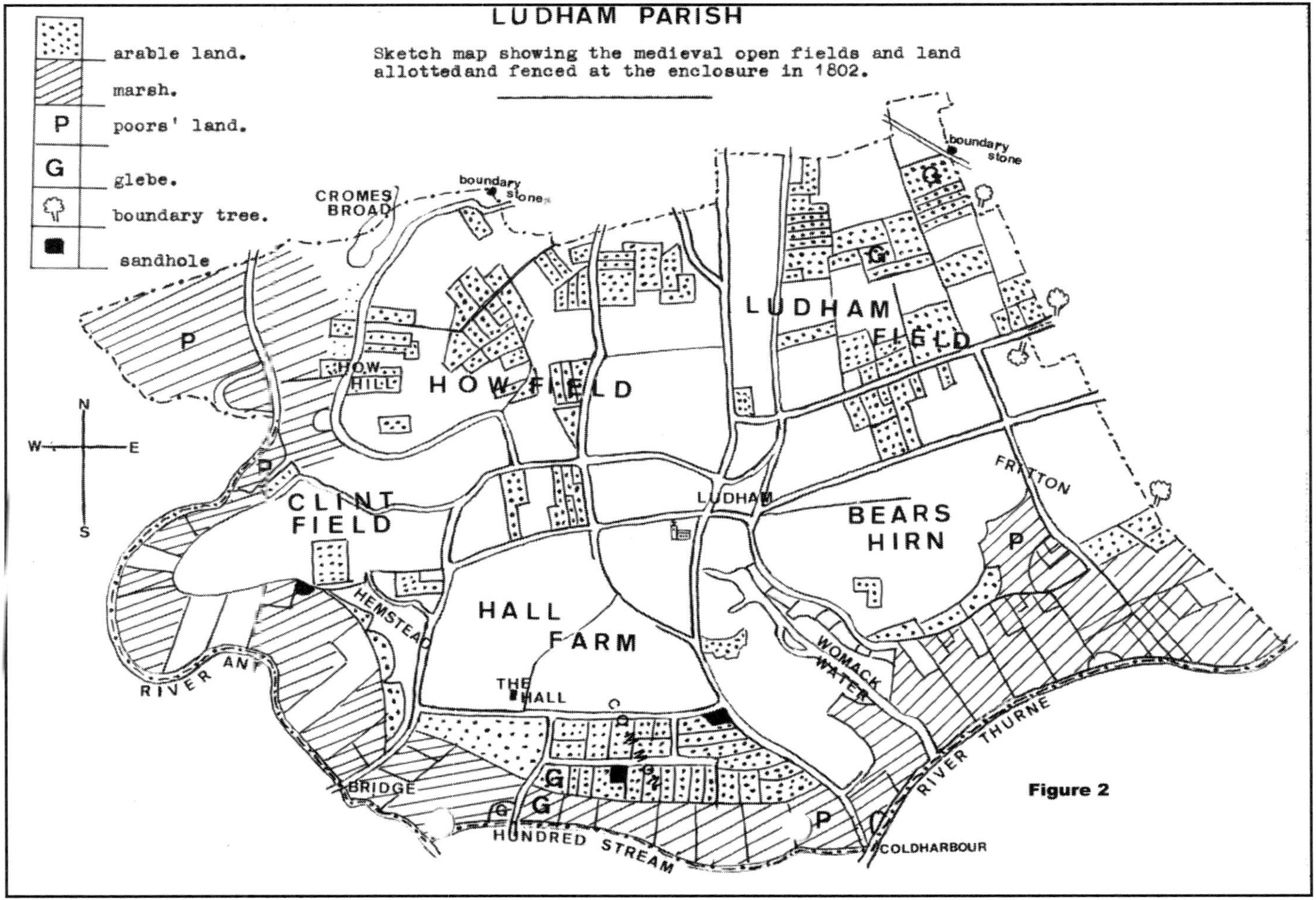
LUDHAM PARISH
Sketch map showing the medieval open fields and land allottedand fenced at the enclosure in 1802.
arable land.
marsh.
P poors' land.
G glebe.
boundary tree.
sandhole
N
W
E
S
CROMES BROAD
boundary stone
boundary stone
HOW HILL
HOW FIELD
LUDHAM FIELD
CLINT FIELD
LUDHAM
BEARS HIRN
FRITTON
HALL FARM
THE HALL
COMMON
HEMSTEAD
WOMACK WATER
RIVER ANT
RIVER THURNE
BRIDGE
HUNDRED STREAM
COLDHARBOUR

Figure 2

to a certain extent, but there are several medieval strips still visible, especially a block of five or six on the Catfield boundary which have been crossed by the making of a bend in the Catfield Road, (which shows incidentally, that the original road north out of Ludham must have been Gipsies Lane). (see Figure 4)

By the mid-eighteenth century agriculture was changing rapidly; roots were being grown as a field crop and drainage of the subsoil was found to improve all crops, but this was not possible unless one had enough land in a single holding.

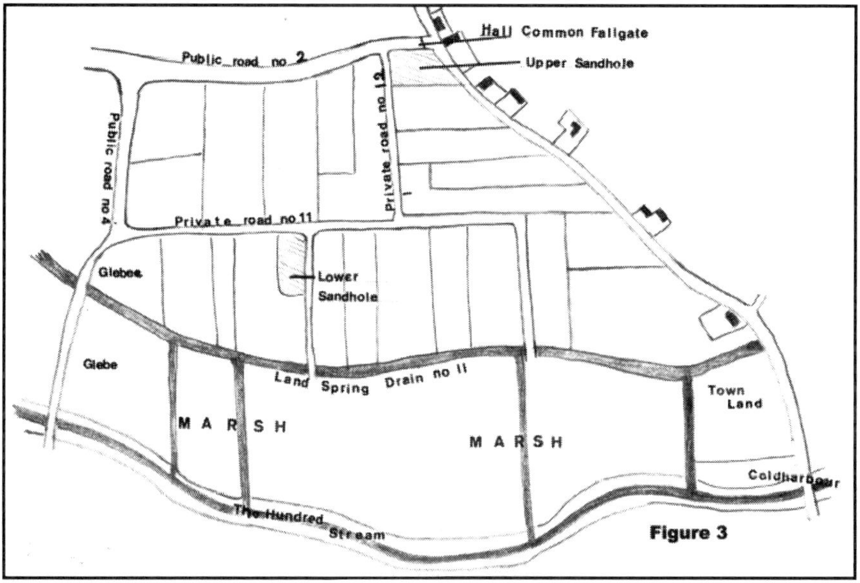

Figure 3. Sketch map showing the common after 1802 divided up and with two private roads giving access. There was a fallgate at Hall Common corner. Today four of the cottages along the road have gone.

Enclosure enhanced the value and increased the production of the land. During the eighteenth century enclosure was mostly by private act of parliament. This was better than enclosure by agreement between owners, but it cost more. 'Agreement' often meant threat of lawsuit. In 1801 came the General Enclosure Act, which simplified and cheapened the proceedings, but the act for Ludham was passed before this, in 1800.

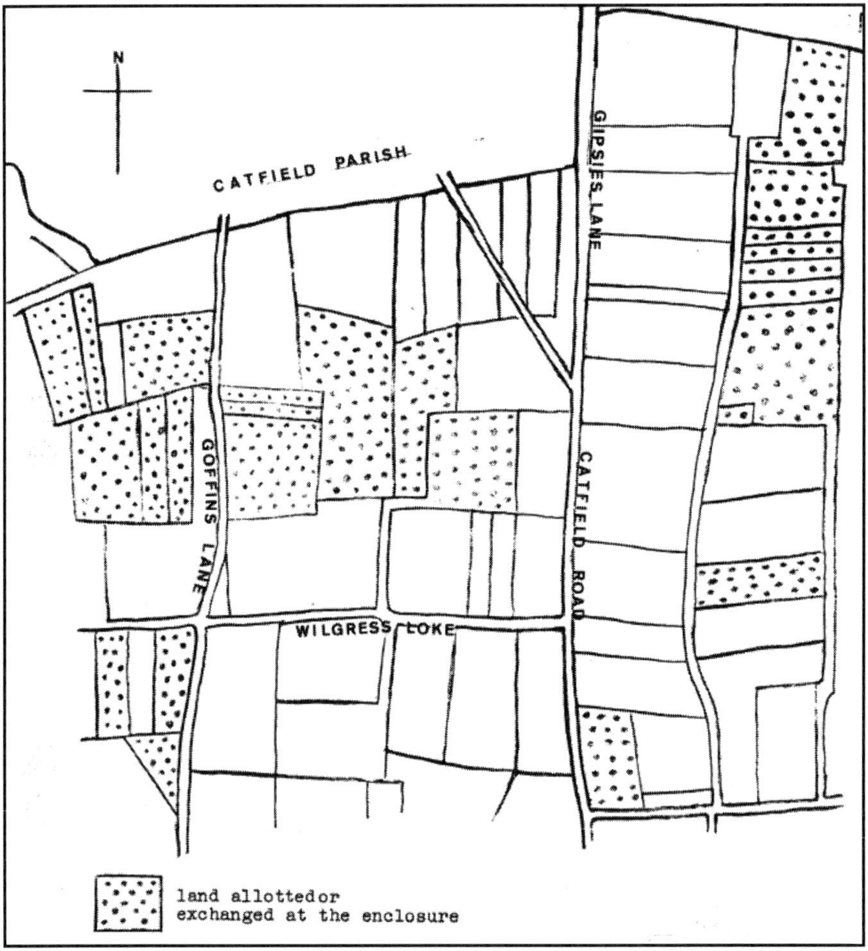

Figure 4. Sketch map of the north centre part of the parish after 1802, showing remains of strips from the old open fields, some allotted and some not. The present Catfield Road crosses a block of strips, showing that it was made later and that Gypsies Lane is the older road northwards. Part of How Hill Field is to the left of the road and part of Ludham Field to the right.

It was an 'Act of Parliament passed in the fortieth year of the Reign of his present Majesty, King George the Third, intituled An Act for dividing, allotting, inclosing, draining and preserving the Open Fields, Commons, Fens and Waste Grounds within the Parish of Ludham in the County of Norfolk'.

The act appointed three General Commissioners; S.G. Ewen, J. Dugmore and J. Futter, whose first move would be to call a public meeting at the Kings Arms. Here they would be sworn in to act impartially and honestly and without favour. A clerk and a surveyor were appointed. Notices were published in the Norfolk Chronicle advertising for all interested persons to set out their claims and describe their holdings, in writing. Similar notices were pinned on the church door and in the local inns for two weeks. Later meetings heard claims, counter-claims and objections. The surveyor got on with measuring with a chain the land, the roads, the banks and ditches and made plans of it all.

The parish boundary would have to be perambulated and verified; the extract from the award opens with a detailed description of it. From it we learn several interesting things; that both the Ant and Thurne were called the North River, (they were once joined by the Hundred Stream); that there is a bit of the old river Ant making a loop in a corner of Reedham Marsh; that Crome's Broad got its name from being allotted to Samuel Crome; that the land directly east of the broad was called Jenny's Heath and had a boundary mark or stone upon it; that there were four boundary trees on the eastern boundary and that where the Hundred Stream joins the Thurne, it is at Ellis' Causeway Gate.

The extract from the award consists of fifteen printed pages, signed by the three commissioners and dated May 28th, 1802. It is concerned with general allotments and not with private individuals and was meant to be kept in the parish. It covers 23 ditches, banks and sock-drains, 3 staithes, 1 boat-dyke, 6 public roads, 18 private roads and 3 sandpits. It also allotted 237 acres of rather marshy land for Poors' Firing. This was to be looked after by the vicar, churchwardens and overseers of the poor and let out by them for the best possible price, the money to be used for buying fuel for certain poor people, and they might also pasture their geese, stock or cattle there. (See Poors' Land Trust)

The six public roads set out and appointed were as follows;

1. The already existing road from Ludham Bridge, across the Hall Fen, to the Fallgate. (By the Dog Inn)
2. Branching east from here to the other Fallgate. (at Hall Common corner) This is a typical enclosure road with wide verges.

3. From the last Fallgate going south-east to Coldharbour.
4. From the middle of no.2 road, south to the Hundred Stream parish boundary.
5. A short stretch of the already existing road from east of Fritton Farm to the Potter boundary. There were two boundary trees here. (Beside a now derelict barn).
6. From the east end of an ancient lane (Willgress Loke) north to the Catfield boundary where it entered 'an old inclosed road'. (This, long since vanished, was the Catfield Old Road, which followed the boundary from Huns Loke to Walton Hall.)

Plate 5. The road from Hall Common to the Dog Inn. Good example of an enclosure road with very wide verges. Photograph, the author

Plate 6.

Boundary tree on the border with Potter Heigham at Green Farm, Fritton. Mentioned in the enclosure award.

Photograph, the author

Plate 7.

All that remained of the Catfield Old Road, along the north-west boundary with Catfield, in about 1965.

Photograph, the author

Of the 18 private roads, three have today become public highways, three others are what used to be called 'byroads' and the rest have either vanished or become grass-grown tracks. The commissioners meant these roads to be private. Most were for 'the use and convenience of the owners and occupiers of land adjoining to the same'. Some were for the vicar and his successors, leading to the glebe. One is solely for the use of Sarah Rust and her heirs or tenants.

There were three sand and gravel pits allotted to the surveyors of highways, two on the common and one at Bluebell Hole. These, with their fences and gates, were to be kept in order by the surveyors and to be used for ever hereafter by them and owners or tenants of land in Ludham for repairing the roads, or as the commissioners for drainage should direct. (The one at Hall Common was for many years the council rubbish tip, but has now been filled in to become allotment gardens.)

The three staithes still exist, at How Hill, Ludham Bridge and Womack. The bridge staithe was moved by the parish council in recent years to the other side of the bridge. The How Hill staithe was almost lost to public use when the Norfolk Education Committee at How Hill tried to claim it and the path leading to it as private, some years ago. There was a public inquiry and the parish council of that time was able to prove, thanks to the extract from the enclosure award, that it was public, to be 'used for ever hereafter as a public staithe by the owners and occupiers of estates within the said parish of Ludham, for the time being, for laying and depositing thereon of the corn, manure and other things which shall be conveyed to and from the common rivers'. The path was one of the private roads, but as well as being for 'the use and convenience of owners and occupiers of land adjoining', was also for 'the several persons who shall be, for the time being be entitled to use the staithe'. Needless to say, we won our case, thanks to Billy Sloper, our parish clerk, who had prepared it all.

Womack Staithe certainly still exists, owned for many years now by the parish council, but the village end of the boat-dyke allotted at the enclosure, running to an old landing place in Staithe Road, was unfortunately lost to public use and wrongly claimed as private at the start of the twentieth century.

The individual printed awards to large and small landowners in the parish were no doubt given to each person, as there were none in the church chest, only the allotment of glebe to the Rev. John Oldershaw, vicar of Ludham and his successors. He was awarded over 24 acres in five holdings, one of which was very small. He was to plant fences and make ditches and keep all in good order.

On the enclosure map from the chest are marked all the allotments and exchanges of land, each one showing the extent in acres, roods and perches, the name of the person concerned and either the name of the person exchanging or the copyhold. The allotments of land are all copyhold of the manor of Ludham except for three, one of Walton Hall manor near How Hill, one of Ludham Bacons manor by the common and one of the manor of Sutton in the south-east corner. This small piece of land could be a relic of medieval times, when, after previous disputes, an agreement was made in 1305 between the Abbot of St. Benets and Lord Abergavenny, (both lords of the manors) that, in future, the Abbot should have two parts and Lord Abergavenny one part of the various profits from Ludham, Catfield and Potter manors. Lord Abergavenny also held the manor of Sutton Outsoken and the manor court was held there one year and at Ludham two years alternately.

In the north-east corner of the parish, Catfield Town Land was allotted over 4 acres, the Potter Heigham glebe a tiny piece of 2r 28p, and the Bethel Hospital in Norwich 6 acres in Ludham and more over the boundary in Potter Heigham.

Of the fourteen people who were allotted more than 10 acres each, the Bishop, as lord of the manor, comes top with over 225 acres. Of this, 53 acres were awarded to him as 'soil', being compensation for his loss of profits from his rights of soil in the commons and wastes. His estate at Ludham Hall stands out as not being affected by the enclosure. It was never part of the open fields, being the demesne farm from medieval times and the property of St. Benets Abbey.

Fourteen other people were allotted less than 10 acres each (See Summary of Awards on page 32). Award of land was based on how much one already owned and the more one had, the more one was allotted.

The common was completely enclosed, being divided between fifteen people and with two new private roads to give access.

The three commissioners end the extract with instructions. The drainage commissioners were to be allowed to enter on the borders of allotments in order to repair, cleanse and scour the ditches and must do as little damage as possible.

The prescribed width of the private roads is set out; they vary from ten, eighteen, nineteen and thirty feet. People whose land touched private or public roads were able to use the grass and herbage growing on them as far as the centre, or right across if they had land both sides. But they must also maintain those roads in good repair and place and maintain stiles, bridges or planks where necessary. No doubt that the enclosure changed the look of the parish. Ditches were to be dug and banks made around most of the allotments. These banks were all to be planted with hawthorn and old hedges were to be trimmed and have the gaps also filled with hawthorn. The farms as we know them now were taking shape, although many hedges have vanished again today.

Plate 8. *Old Ludham Bridge. The staithe was originally on the right.*
Old Postcard

We do not know the cost of the enclosure. It was borne by people in proportion to the amount of land that they received. There was a lot to be paid for; the wages of the three commissioners, the surveyor, the clerk and probably a solicitor, journeys, chaise and horse hire, bills for the inns, newspaper notices, printing, letter writing, stamps, land sale expenses, ditching and fencing. The cost of banking and hedging even a small piece of land would have been quite heavy, so many poorer men would have sold their little plot rather than pay. Thus the smaller farmers disappeared.

There is a comment on the Ludham enclosure in the 'General View of the Agriculture of the County of Norfolk' by Arthur Young, published in 1804. It says; 'The commons were enclosed in 1801: all cottagers that claimed, had allotments and one for the fuel to the whole, but the cottages did not belong to the poor; the allotments in general went to the larger proprietors, and the poor consequently were left, in this respect, destitute: many cows were kept before, few now. All the poor very much against the measure'.

There is a further comment by Mr. Cubitt of Catfield, who farmed land in both parishes. He had the second largest allotment in Ludham after the Bishop. Mr. Cubitt thought 'that where enclosing has converted land to arable, the poor get as much by gleaning as they did by the common: the high price of cattle has lessened the number of their cows: geese and fuel have of late been their chief advantage; nor, does he remark, that those who support themselves by commons, are richer or better off than others depending on the labour of the farmers'.

It is difficult to judge the extent of hardship in Ludham due to the enclosure. There were no documents relating to the poor between 1787 and 1825. By the time of the 1851 census – 49 years afterwards – there were 127 men employed on farms and 2 out-of-work pauper labourers. So by then the larger farms were providing the main employment in the parish.

Sources:

W.E. Tate. The Parish Chest. 1946 - Cambridge University Press.

W.E. Tate. The English Village Community and the Enclosure Movement. 1967 - Victor Gollancz Ltd.

Summary of Enclosure Awards, 1802

Land is measured in acres, roods and perches

		Awarded:		
The Hall	Bishop of Norwich	225 acres plus		
Catfield	George Cubitt	143	"	"
	Isaac Horsley	123	"	"
Johnson St.	Wm. Clopton Johnson	88	"	"
	John Manning	71	"	"
	Thomas Cook	65	"	"
Horsefen Rd.	Roger Harrison	62	"	"
Whitegate Fm.	James Garrett	59	"	"
	Mary Brown	53	"	"
	Sarah Rust	42	"	"
Cromes Farm	Samuel Crome	37	"	"
Fritton	Rebecca Rayley	24	"	"
	Mary Ann Page	17	"	"
	J. Ditcham	10	"	"

Less than 10 acres:
Elizabeth Harwood, Robert Howard, William Roll, Foster Bradford William Green, Thomas Smith, Jasper Deeker, Ann Donne, Thomas Marston, William Kidman, J.B. Crow, Sarah Pettingle, Robert Hollis, Meadows Frost.

Various:

Vicar's glebe	awarded	24a	2r	10p
Catfield Town Land	awarded	4a	0r	2p
Heigham glebe	awarded	0a	3r	28p
Bethel Hospital	awarded	6a	0r	25p

Poors' Land Trust:

The Hulver	awarded	33a	1r	37p
Gt. Reedham	awarded	85a	0r	0p
Turf Fen	awarded	11a	2r	4p
Cold Harbour	awarded	6a	3r	39p

Others:

23 drains, banks and dykes	3 staithes
1 boat dyke	6 public roads
18 private roads	3 sand and gravel pits

Total Acreage of Parish from White's Directory	2977
Total approximate acreage awarded	1325

Note: It is interesting to see that there are seven women farming, four of them on quite a large scale.

1804, The Agricultural Review by Arthur Young

Farming was very prosperous during the 18th century and many of the big barns in Ludham were built during this time. In the 1790's Norfolk was exporting more grain than all the rest of the country. At the beginning of the 19th century the price of wheat was high, due to the Napoleonic wars. The war stimulated farming more than ever, and it was also a time of enclosure when marsh and common were being divided up and waste land was coming into cultivation. Farms were improving with the acquisition and exchange of land, enabling them to have all the land together instead of scattered pieces all over the parish.

The farmers' aim was to increase fertility without over cropping. There was much experimenting with various substances to fertilise the land, other than the traditional farmyard manure. Each farmer was his own scientist and had his theories about fertilisers. Among the most popular was marle, a type of clay. This came to Ludham by boat from Thorpe and Whitlingham. It cost 4 shillings a chaldron and in Ludham they put eight to ten cartloads on an acre with a long lasting effect. Ludham was very convenient for water transport with three staithes and plenty of river bank.

Fields were being drained now, not with pipes, but with drains of brushwood or stones. The use of the drill for sowing seeds was become widespread, but not all farmers were convinced of its use; many still broadcast or dibbled seeds, but the latter needed a lot of labour. Often women were employed for this, as it was fiddling work, dropping three seeds into each hole! Children were best at it.

Threshing used to be done in the barns, by two men with flails - a tool in use since biblical times. Then the corn was winnowed by being thrown across the barn with a wooden shovel and the draught between the two doors blew away the chaff and colder which was lighter than the corn, which was why barns always had two opposite doors. Then came the invention of the threshing mill, worked by horses walking round and round. This was a great improvement, although much more expensive than by flail. There was a threshing mill in one of the barns at Beeches Farm.

Plate 9. Two of the barns at Beeches Farm, dated 1745 and 1797. Taken for the author in 1967 by Broadland Photographers.

A Board of Agriculture was established by William Pitt in 1793 and this commissioned a series of reports on the agriculture of each county. A review of Norfolk by N. Kent was published in 1796 and later revised by Arthur Young, himself secretary to the Board, in 1804. This was to be followed later by William Marshall's review in 1818. Young's was a tremendous undertaking and it is fascinating to read today. He rode all over Norfolk calling on about sixty farmers in different areas and noting every aspect of their farms, buildings, implements, crops, cattle etc.

In Ludham he visited Mr. William Hornard, a successful and go-ahead farmer. He poses us a problem today. We do not know which was his farm, and Young does not tell us. One would have imagined that he would be at Ludham Hall, the most important farm in the parish, but a list of tenants from 1760 to 1851 does not include him. The only thing we do know is that he and his wife and infant son are buried beneath a fine black marble slab just in front of the lectern in Ludham church. From this we can work out that he was born in 1747 and from his discussion with Arthur Young we know that he began farming in Ludham 28 years previously, i.e. in 1772 when he was about 25. His wife died in 1796 and no doubt Young was gathering information soon after that and must have talked to him then. The Enclosure took place in Ludham in 1801-1802 and involved all the landowners but there is absolutely no mention of Mr. Hornard, so by this time he must have moved to Hingham, where he may have had relatives - (White's directory gives a Rev. W. B. H. Hurnard at Gurneys Manor there in 1845) - and where, according to his tombstone, he died in 1821 aged 74.

Be that as it may, Mr Hornard was farming somewhere in Ludham for over 30 years.

Arthur Young said that the soil of East Norfolk was amongst the finest in the kingdom, with clay marle easily available by boat. There also the vast marshes were an asset, not only for grazing large herds of cattle, but for all the sedge and rushes which were used for bedding cattle in the yards, thus making manure. On this Mr Hornard remarked that when the sea broke through the marram banks and flooded the marshes, some years previously, he had a loss of about 60 or 70 loads of rushes in a year and could

Plate 10. A fine barn, which stood at the top of the hill on the Yarmouth Road, unfortunately demolished in the 1960s. Photograph taken for the author in 1967 by Broadland Photographics.

not make enough manure because of it. In Ludham farmers put at least twelve loads of manure on an acre, Mr Hornard often putting on twenty loads and he never kept it longer than a year on the muck heap. Other fertilisers tried out among many, were oyster shells, pond weed, ashes, malt dust and town manure from Yarmouth.

Mr Hornard was the first in the area to try “tathing” the wheat fields. Arthur Young had never seen this before and thought it a "singular husbandry". It consisted of carting turnips onto the young wheat in February and March, then putting sheep or bullocks on the field to feed. This gave heavy crops of wheat with stiff straw. Around Ludham and Catfield they produced 7 to 8 coombs an acre. Mr Hornard used all his turnip crop in this way, carting them on to his layers and wheat stubble as well as onto the wheat. His bullocks always fed out in the fields; "ten beasts at liberty make as much manure as thirty tied up" he said, but he brought them in at night onto hay or straw.

The crop rotation in Ludham was the then common five shift: 1 Turnips, 2 Barley, 3 Clover, 4 Wheat, and 5 Barley. In Happing Hundred it was said that if one grew clover too often it did not do well, and one had to use a six shift rotation and mix the white clover with trefoil and ray grass. Mr Hornard did not agree and said that he had sowed clover every five years for the last 28 years and that each crop was as good as the last.

Mr Hornard was still dibbling a part of his crops and sowing the rest broadcast; he was not sure which was the best. The seed drill, still quite a novelty, was more in use in West Norfolk than in the east, apart from a few in the Fleggs, but it was soon to be universal, for the straw was stiffer and the ears longer of drilled corn, and crops sown in drills could later be horse or hand-hoed easily.

Another old custom dying out at this time was the use of oxen as working beasts. They were being used less as they were difficult to shoe and the men were prejudiced against their use. In Happing, Young said there were five horses used for every 100 acres.

Plate 11. Old farm waggon belonging to Clifford Kittle.
Taken for the author in 1967 by Broadland Photographics.

If the farmers and bigger landowners were prospering at the start of the 19th century, the situation was very different for the farm labourers. Because of the long war with France, the high price of provisions, wool, leather etc, made it difficult for a poor man with a young family to keep them either fed or warm without assistance. In Happing a labourer earned about two shillings a day. Some farmers let their men have cheap corn at five shillings a bushel. By 1806 many were half-starved and the recent enclosure had not helped with the loss of the common land. It had also forced many to sell their only piece of land, as they could not afford to fence it as required. Prices did not fall as expected after the end of the war in 1815 and then the Corn Law prevented the importation of cheaper corn. Farm labourers began to riot, burning stacks and breaking machinery. Ludham seems to have escaped this, and again in 1830 when there were widespread riots in over 150 Norfolk parishes.

Thus agriculture at the beginning of the 19th century; the farming community completely divided in two, farmers were prospering and producing more and better crops and their labourers were becoming paupers and desperate.

Sources:
David & Charles reprint 1969 of "General View of the Agriculture of the County of Norfolk" by Arthur Young, 1804.
"An Historical Atlas of Norfolk", 1993, Norfolk Museum Services

1814, A Commercial Calling Card

Some years ago Daphne Fuller discovered in Fritton farmhouse a small card. It was the commercial calling card of a tailor from Gt. Yarmouth. He did the rounds of the villages, waiting in the local inn for clients to come to him, having distributed his cards in advance. Mr W. Roe must have made quite a few uniforms as the war with France had been going on for twenty years, but six months after the date of his card the Battle of Waterloo would take place.

naval and military
UNIFORMS

ROE,
tailor & draper,
market place,
Yarmouth,

HATS , GLOVES
AND
HOSIERY.

Lodgings
Keymer, Printer.

(not the original lettering)

On the reverse side is printed:

"W. Roe, For the accommodation of his Friends, intends himself the pleasure of waiting upon them at the Kings Arms Inn, Ludham on Thursday the 5th January 1815 and will continue his visits the 1st Thursday in every ensuing Month and humbly solicits their patronage and support.

Yarmouth 24th Dec. 1814."

(See page 145 for Mrs. Fuller's other find at Fritton Farm.)

1821, An Early Methodist Chapel

We do not know just how or when the Wesleyan Methodists began to be active in Ludham. In a Register of Meeting Houses there is the following entry, dated 10 January 1801; "certified by Gabriel Smith, schoolmaster, that in a dwelling house of William Clopton Johnson, a certain low room, now used as a schoolroom, to be set aside for the exercise of religious worship for divers of H.M. Protestant subjects dissenting from the Church of England". It is fairly certain that W.C.Johnson lived in Johnson Street, named after him. He was a prosperous farmer and all his land was around that area. He very probably lived in Stone House, once a farm, having three barns beside it on estate maps of 1824 and 1828.

Was this "low room" the earliest Methodist Meeting place in Ludham? In a plan of the Yarmouth circuit dated 1816, Ludham is mentioned as a Society and preachers were appointed.

By 1821 a room was presumably not large enough and it was decided to build a proper chapel. On April 24 of that year, Sarah Rust, a widow, sold a piece of land "next to a certain road called Baldwyns" to the Rev. William Bacon, the Superintendent Minister, for the sum of £5.

Baldwyns Lane, later called Grimes Lane and now, Malthouse Lane, runs from The Street, alongside Albury House until it joins Latchmoor Lane. Here the first chapel was built. It was 28 feet long and 24 feet wide.

The History of Wesleyan Methodism in Gt. Yarmouth by W.L.Mack, gives a brief description of the interior; "It was square with side and front galleries. The pulpit was a high and uncomfortable box where you could shake hands with those in the side galleries. There was a small choir but a good one who could read music fairly well". This chapel was opened in November 1821 and was in regular use for 45 years and the cause grew steadily till it became necessary to build a bigger chapel elsewhere, this one not being large enough.

The Trustees of this first chapel were:

James Norton of Stokesby	farmer
Edward Rice of Ludham	marshman
John Beverly of Martham	shoemaker
Martin Sandall of Ludham	farmer
John Thurgate of Ludham	shoemaker
William Carrier of Rollesby	farmer
Robert Beverly of Martham	farmer
George Simpson of Yarmouth	shoemaker
James Spanson of Yarmouth	tailor.

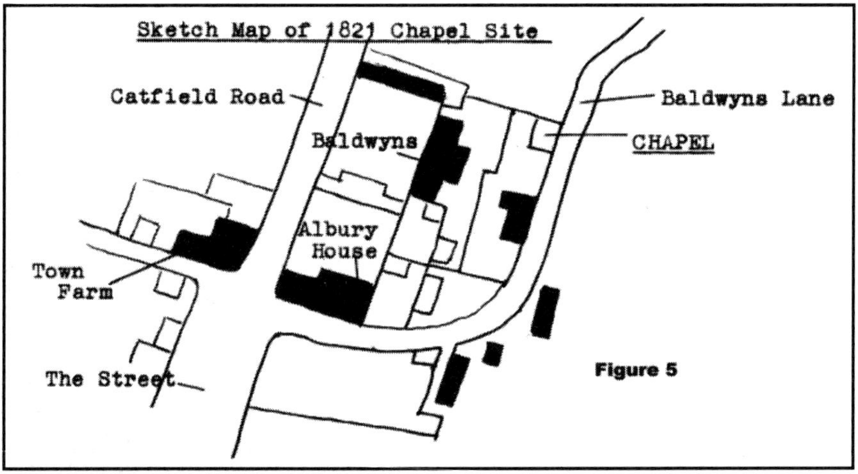

Figure 5

On 4 July 1866 permission was given by the President of the Conference of People Called Methodists to sell the chapel and its land in Baldwyn's Lane. Conditions were laid down that, when it was sold, it must not be used as a place of worship, nor a public house, nor yet a beer house, or the land and building would revert to the Trustees. John Chaplin, a builder, bought it for £35, took possession and turned it into a stable. In 1904 there is a reference to “a chapel or meeting house, formerly a stable, now a mill”.

Sources:
Booklet of Centenary of the High St. Methodist Church, 1967, sent to me by Bill Sloper.
Deeds of Folly House (Baldwyns) lent to me by the late William Mervyn.
Register of Meeting Houses 1758, N.R.O.

1821, The Baptist Chapel

There was a Baptist chapel in Ludham in Staithe Road, about halfway between Staithe House and The Mowle, on the opposite side of the road. The field to the south of it was called Meeting House Pightle.

There were two sorts of Baptists; the General, for general redemption, and the Strict and Particular, where only some people could be saved. Baptism was for believers only and consisted of total immersion.

The Ludham chapel, built in 1821 to seat 150 people, was the Strict and Particular. It was demolished in 1975 and new houses have been built there.

Plate 12. Ludham Baptist Chapel from the South. Photograph by the author c.1965

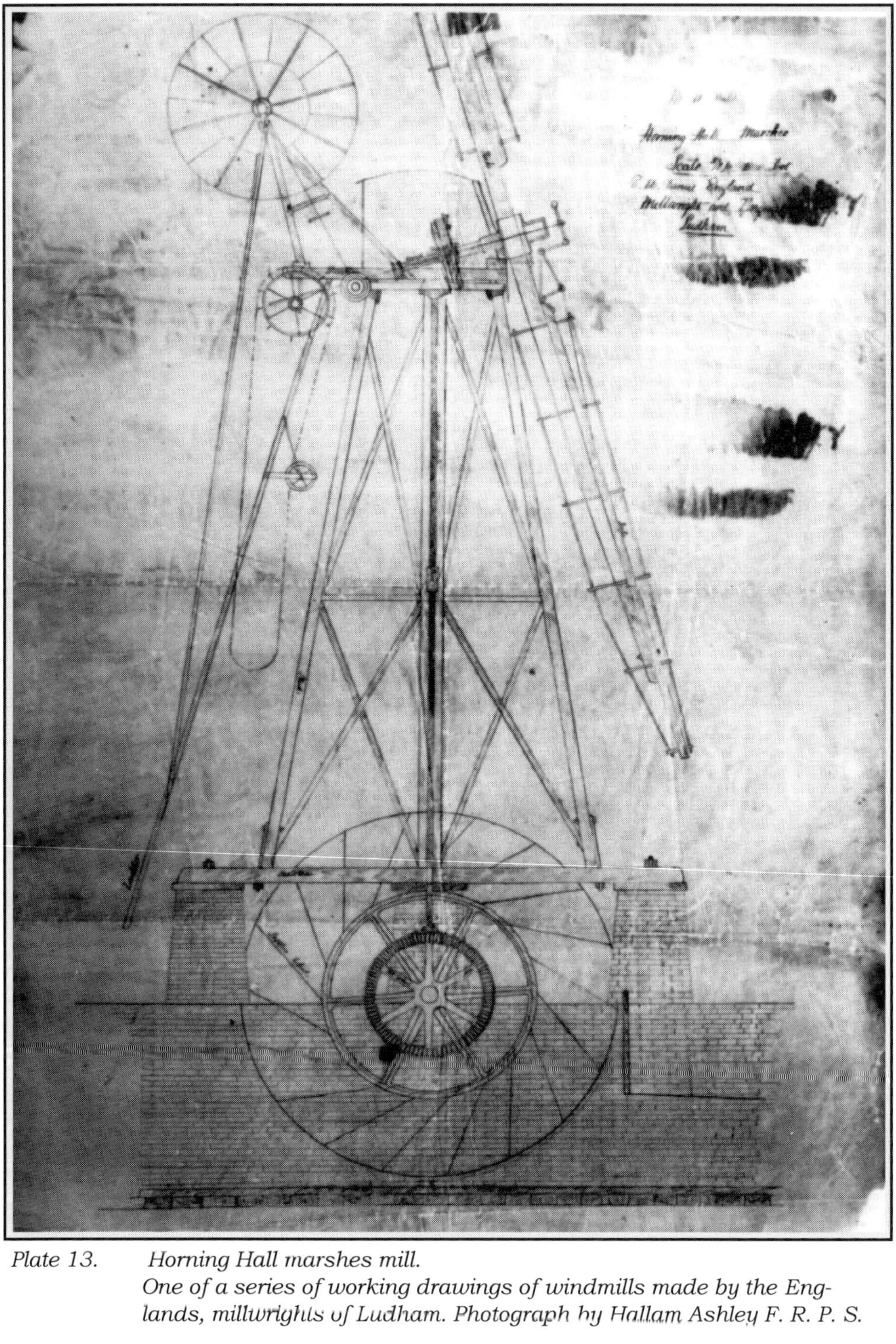

Plate 13. Horning Hall marshes mill.
One of a series of working drawings of windmills made by the Englands, millwrights of Ludham. Photograph by Hallam Ashley F. R. P. S.

1830, The England Family: Millwrights

The Englands were millwrights and engineers in Ludham for almost two hundred years. Their workshops were extensive wooden buildings, which covered nearly three-quarters of an acre in the centre of the village on the west side. There were two saw pits and the Street must have been very busy with teams of horses hauling tree trunks to be sawn and other horses with carts transporting everything. The workshops were all demolished in 1937 after the decline in the use of wind power.

Already in the eighteenth century there were David England, born 1715, John, born 1740 and William, born 1770, all millwrights.

At the beginning of the nineteenth century William was associated in business with William Cubitt, who invented patent sails for windmills in 1807. These had moveable shutters in the sails, which replaced the old cloth sails. The Englands made great use of this invention and the first mills to be equipped with patent sails were Cooke's smock mill at Stalham and Jonathan Nickerson's old post mill at Horning, the latter fitted by William England. These patent sails later became common all over the country.

William Cubitt, whose wife was a Ludham woman, Abigail Sparkhall, had his workshops in Horning Lower Street. He was later knighted by Queen Victoria for his work as chief construction engineer for the Crystal Palace. He also did a major work at Lowestoft harbour when it became silted up, at a cost of £80,000.

In 1830 William England died at his home on the west side of Ludham Street, almost next to the workshops. He left a son, another William, born in 1806 and a daughter, Sarah, born in 1801. Sarah had two illegitimate sons, William Kirby, born in 1821 and Daniel Chasteney, born in 1823.

By 1851 William and his sister Sarah, both still unmarried, were still living in the same house with William' s 17-year old daughter, Harriet England, and Sarah's son William Kirby, then a journeyman millwright of 29.

There was also an apprentice millwright, Robert Newton. Sarah's other son, Daniel Chasteney had married Harriet Smith, a Norwich dressmaker, in March 1850, and they lived just opposite. Daniel later lived in the house on the Catfield Road now known as Folly House. His wife died giving birth to their daughter Laura in 1859. He later married Elizabeth, a cook from Horning Hall. By 1883 they had become landlords at the Kings Arms, where they built up a good reputation for hospitality.

Daniel and his brother William Kirby carried on the very successful millwright and engineering business with their uncle, William. It could be dangerous work and William Kirby was badly injured in an accident at a mill in 1856 and died from his injuries the following year, aged only 36. His widow, a Ludham woman born Harriot Fairhead, obtained compensation and with the money she opened a grocery shop in the thatched house at the north end of Ludham Street. (Later Cook's shop, it had been a farmhouse previously.)

Daniel invented a turbine apparatus, which drained the marshes far better than the old scoop wheel. He adapted his turbine for use by horse, steam or wind. The first one went into use on Horsey Marshes around 1867. Daniel also introduced the patent sails into Denmark and a fantail for turning the mill into the wind.

The Englands did all the drainage work in Ludham. There were once six drainage mills on the extensive marshes around the parish. Englands also worked for the Ecclesiastical Commissioners and several other large landowners like Lord Somerleyton and Sir Thomas Beauchamp of Loddon and Langley. Their windmills were all over Norfolk.

After Daniel's death in 1897 his son Edwin William Daniel England, who was millwright, mechanical engineer and pump manufacturer, took over both the works and the Kings Arms and continued well into the beginning of the twentieth century.

All that survives now is a collection of working drawings of windmills by the Englands. They are beautiful and are thought to be the only nineteenth century working drawings in the country. They were photographed in 1968 by the late Hallam Ashley, before being sent to the London Record Office. Mr Ashley, knowing my interest in Ludham, kindly gave me a set and it is one of these that is reproduced here. It shows the mill on Horning Hall marshes and it was drawn by Edwin William Daniel, one of the last of the millwrights. (Plate 13)

Sources:
Chesney England, Ludham, descendant of the millwright family, whose own father was killed in a mill accident at Lambrigg Mill, Waxham, in 1920.
Rex Wailes, The English Windmill, 1954, Routledge & Keegan Paul.
Rex Wailes, Norfolk Windmills, part II Drainage Mills. Newcomen Society Transactions, vol 30, pages 157-177, 1955-57

Plate 14. *High Mill, Ludham. Probably built about 1800 by William England. Very low tower, sails turned clockwise. This replaced an earlier post mill. (Ludham Mill) - Old Postcard*

Plate 15. Catfield Post Mill. A good example of the type of mill that stood in Ludham originally; the Town Mill in Love Lane and Ludham Mill at the top of Old Mill Loke. Old Postcard

Ludham Windmills

Corn Mills.

High Mill, known as Ludham Mill - TG 397186

There is some doubt about the date of the present mill. An article in the Eastern Daily Press in 1932 when the mill was made into a garage, gave the date as 1742, but this seems too early. In a letter to me in 1973, Harry Apling, author of "Norfolk Corn Windmills" wrote, "it would now seem that the date 1742 might relate to the building of the post mill by David England, born 1715, and that the tower mill would not be earlier than about 1800, being built by William England". The earlier post mill stood nearer the top of Old Mill Lane.

Arthur Newton, born 1886, remembered, " this mill had sails which turned clockwise. It had a very short tower and the sails were very low and used to pass over one door, so you had to go out the other one. Billy Slaughter's father was struck by the sails once! The wind could be very strong up there. The mill measured 21 feet across the bottom floor. Very thick walls. It was lovely and warm in there. When 10 or 11 years old, I used to be up there while father went to get the beer".

How Hill Mill -TG374191

Is on the O.S. 1837 map and mentioned in tithe schedule as "mill, house etc, James Page". House and mill were built by William Sherwood Page in 1825, although the actual construction work was probably done by Englands. It worked until 1890 the sails being taken down in 1893.

The Town Mill - TG 387178

On the 1802 enclosure map. Was situated in Love Lane, at end of The Homestead garden. Shape still visible in 1960's. It was a post mill, driving two pairs of stones. Very damaged in the great gale of 1896. Repaired afterwards, but destroyed by fire on Dec. 1st 1896.

The deeds date from 1699.

Drainage Mills.

Horse Fen Mill - TG 408176

Near Potter Heigham boundary by the River Thurne. Brick tower with patent sails and scoop wheel. Built by Englands, date unknown.

Womack Water Mill - TG400175

On the marshes at the end of Horsefen Road. Brick tower and cloth sails. All-wood windshaft.

Coldharbour Mill - TG 397168

At Coldharbour, left of the road, on a marsh once called Flash Pightle. Now only visible as a slight bump by the river bank. Brick tower with a pitched roof over the scoop wheel. Built by Englands.

Ludham Bridge, north -TG 372172

About 150 yards upstream from the bridge. Brick tower, was used as gun post and look-out during the 1939-45 war as it was at the edge of the coastal defence area.

Ludham Bridge, south - TG 374169

About 200 yards downstream from the bridge. Built by Englands. Scoop wheel. Demolished 1930's. Now only 4 red brick support piers remain, with iron wheel on spindle to concrete pump shaft.

How Hill Mill. - TG370192

A little upstream from the staithe. Open framework timber tower on 4 brick piers. Internal ladder, windshaft. Built by Englands, March 1897 to replace an older one. Restored by Norfolk Windmill Trust.

(Drainage Windmills of the Norfolk Marshes by Arthur C. Smith. Stevenage Museum Publications. 1978)

Plate 16.

Drainage Mill south of Ludham Bridge. Photograph, the author

1841, The Church School and Earlier Schools

There were certainly "dame" schools in private houses before the advent of organised education in Ludham, and an early reference to this type of school is found in a register of Meeting Houses.

On January 10, 1801 , Gabriel Smith, a schoolmaster, certified that "a certain low room in the house of William Clopton Johnson, now used as a schoolroom, was to be set aside for the exercise of religious worship...". We do not know if this room was to be used exclusively for religious purposes or whether it continued to be used as a schoolroom on weekdays. Nor do we know for sure where this house was, but W. C. Johnson, a fairly big landowner, had all his farmland in the Johnson Street area, so the only possible house of any size there is Stone House, which was once a farm with barns beside it.

After this date there are references to more schoolmasters resident in Ludham. It is not known how long each was here as their names occur mostly in Registers of Baptisms, when their children are christened, and sometimes on other documents, as presumably not all were married. Benjamin Hastings is the first. He is mentioned in 1810 and 1815, He occurs also as the valuer of the goods of a deceased person in 1817 and is concerned with a lease in 1823. Next is Daniel Graves with only one mention, in 1832.

About this time a daily school had started in a house hired for the purpose, its whereabouts unknown. 53 children were receiving instruction here but the accommodation was not at all convenient. Two schoolmasters were resident in the parish at this time; Charles Townsend and Thomas Clark were both here between 1834 and 1841. One of them had been obtained from the Diocesan Training School at Norwich.

The Parliamentary Gazetteer for the Parish of Ludham, Norfolk, established in 1843-44 by A. Fullerton & Co, London, states that "there are six daily schools", but gives no details.

By 1841 it was decided to build a proper schoolroom in Ludham, and the vicar, the Rev. W.A. Bathhurst, notified the National Society for Promoting Religious Education of this intention. The site chosen was part of the extensive churchyard and a faculty was applied for. The Society advised against this on the grounds of unnecessary expense and also because it precluded the possibility of any grant from the government which did not recognise such a document as legal security of tenure. However, the parish decided to go ahead as planned. The proposed school-room was to be built of brick with a slate roof and to measure 38½ feet by 19½ feet, providing 125 places, allowing 6sq feet per child, which was the minimum stipulated by the Society.

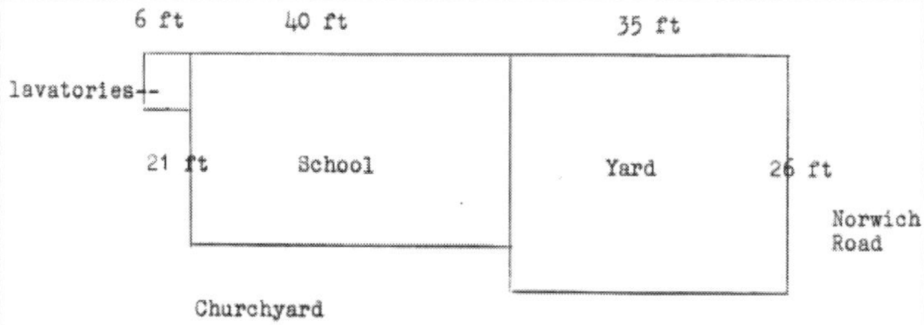

Figure 6 Plan from the faculty.

This old school stood on the site of the present Church Room, and the faculty allows that it was built a little larger than needed by the Society's recommendations, being 40 feet by 21 feet, with a yard in front, towards the road, of 35 feet by 26 feet and 6 sq. feet at the rear for lavatories. There was no door to the churchyard. The roof is just visible in an old photograph of the Norwich Road, or Church Street, as it was called then. The present Church Room was made out of the old school building around the beginning of this century, and it took in the school yard as well. The exact size of the old school may still be seen today in the narrower end of the Church Room, and the toilets are on the site of the old earth closets.

The cost of the school was estimated at £155 and by the end of March 1841, £110 had been raised locally, with contributions from certain well-disposed persons. The National Society contributed £30 to make up the total and the building was completed and paid for by March 1842.

The school was to be conducted upon the principles of the National Society for the education of the poor in the principles of the established church. At the time of the National Society's

Church School Enquiry in 1846-47, 55 boys and 50 girls were attending the daily school. Of this number, all but 2 boys and 1 girl attended also on Sundays, and there were, in addition, 7 boys and 4 girls who attended on Sundays only. The children were taught by a master and an assistant mistress who received a joint salary of £40 per year, and the total expenditure of the school was estimated at £55 per year. The charge for instruction was one penny a week for labourers' children, twopence a week for journeymens' children and threepence for those of tradesmen.

By 1857 the brick floor was in a bad condition and needed replacing, but unfortunately it was not possible to obtain any government aid towards the cost, because of the unacceptable tenure of the site. The vicar, now the Rev. A. Walker, advised the National Society that, apart from the childrens' pence he received no help towards the expenses of the school and that the previous year he had paid the teacher's salary of £31, which amounted to one tenth of his whole income. New books were required also and he could do no more.

Unknown to the National Society, the faculty contained the stipulation that the Society should be responsible for keeping the schoolroom in good repair. However, all the Society's available income was committed to building purposes and therefore it could not come to the rescue as Mr Walker had hoped. He was recommended to contact the S.P.C.K., which at that time was assisting the work of voluntary schools and also the National Society, by giving grants for books etc, but there is no record of thc outcome of Mr Walker's application. The Church School must have continued for a lot longer, in spite of difficulties, for it is mentioned in a rate book of 1879, along with the new Board School, which had just come into being in 1873.

Going back to 1851, we find on the census returns of that year, a schoolmaster living in the first house on the Yarmouth Road, (today it contains a gift shop). He was Hiram Coustos, aged 30, who came from Yarmouth, and his wife, Sarah, aged 39, a schoolmistress, born in New Buckenham. Living in the house with them were three young pupil boarders; 5 year old Reuben Garrett of Hickling, 5 year old Thomas Bryant of Ipswich and 6 year old Mary Ann Kipper from Fleggburgh. Martha Fordham, a 26-year-old general servant, also lived with them. Coustos was also a general agent for servants and an agent for the Temperance and

General Provident Institution. Hunt's directory of 1850 shows Coustos with the word "school" and Richard Lincoln as the National Schoolmaster, so presumably Coustos ran his school on his own, while Lincoln taught at the Church School. However, Hiram Coustos seems to have died young, for, according to a rate book of 1852, Mrs Coustos is a widow. Did she go on teaching at her little school until she was over 60? Mr. Charles George, born in 1867, told me that he went to the present Ludham School on the first day that it opened in 1873, but that, before that, he went to school in a house in the Yarmouth Road, was taught by an old lady and that he paid one penny a week for his education....
It would be interesting to see from a register of burials just when Sarah Coustos died.

Sources:
I am very grateful to the National Society for Promoting Religious Education for the most helpful letter that they wrote to me in 1973 concerning the Church School.
Register of Meeting Houses, 1758. Norfolk Record Office.
Register of Baptism, Ludham, 1813-41.
Faculty for Church School, Ludham, 1841.
Hunt's Directory, 1850.
Census Returns for Ludham, 1851.

Plate 17. Church Street (the Norwich Road), showing the Church School in the centre by the figure, with a chimney on the west side. When it became the present Church Room it was enlarged towards the road. Old Postcard.

1842, The Commutation of Tithes

The payment of tithes was a very ancient custom that had existed in England since well before the Norman Conquest. Tithe, an old English word, means a tenth, which was the portion of all produce to be paid to the church, the clergy and the poor. Like all compulsory payments, it caused many disputes, especially as it had to be paid in kind. The great tithes were of corn, hay and wool and all other produce was the small tithe. Imagine the nuisance of having to calculate a tenth part of one's produce and then having to deliver it to the church porch or the parsonage. And the arguments, if the hens were scrawny or the hay a bit mouldy.... So it was not surprising that there was a general demand for tithes to be commuted, or changed, into money payments.

In Ludham the Hall Farm lands had never paid tithe. This was because they had once belonged to the nearby monastery of St Benets Abbey. In 1220 the church revenues had been appropriated to the abbey, which meant, amongst other things, that the abbot became rector of the parish and took the great tithes, while the parish priest became vicar and had only the small tithes. The vicar was compensated for this by receiving the corn-tithes and other revenue from an area of land, which stretched from the Boat Dyke (by Staithe House) right down to Coldharbour. This took in large parts of Hall Common Farm and Manor Farm to a total of 69 acres of arable and 39 acres of marsh. It was known as Reedcroft or the Goose Croft Lands. In the second church register there is an explanation of this, written in 1706, following a list of glebe land:

"Besides these, all the Great or Corn tithes arising out of certain lands in Ludham extending from the Boatfleet or Running-Stock to Coldharbour, called Reedcroft, the greatest part is now in the occupation of Thomas Haddon of Ludham, gent, belonging to the vicar of Ludham aforesaid, also the tithe of Hay, Clover, Turneps, Wool and Lamb: and also twelve pence Herbage for every acre of feeding ground or pasture in lieu of Cow and Calf. And also ten shillings per annum for the corn-mill of Ludham, which now is and time out of mind, hath been paid to the vicar as a Modus or Composition for the same. And also the tithe of Wood and all other tithes and Duties Ecclesiastical throughout the whole parish, (except the tithes of Corn other than those of Reedcroft aforesaid, and also except the tithes and herbages arising out of the Hall-lands, which the Occupiers thereof claim discharged from payment thereof by virtue of the Act for dissolving Monasteries) which said tithes are by the said vicar yearly taken in kind or Composition for the same."

It is interesting to note that the vicar was already receiving some of his tithes in cash over a hundred years before the act of parliament to commute tithes.

On Saturday 6 October, 1838 there appeared an advertisement in The Norfolk Chronicle and Norwich Gazette, among several other similar ones, regarding a meeting of land-owners and tithe-owners to be held at the Kings Arms on 15 October at 11 a.m. (See Fig: 7.) They were to meet to discuss the commutation of tithes following the provisions of an act of parliament passed in 1836. A survey of the parish would be made by an official valuer and would result in the publication of the tithe map and schedule for Ludham. A copy of each was kept in the church chest. It also followed that the tithes in kind were at last commuted into fixed rent-charges for each plot of land. This rent was based upon average corn prices during the previous seven years.

It is a large scale map, full of interesting information. Every field and dwelling is shown, all are numbered and the schedule shows the owner, occupier, description, use and exact acreage. It is also an excellent source of field names

On page 49 is a sketch map of the village centre with some of the inhabitants marked on it, taken from the tithe schedule. It shows a busy village full of trade and industry and self-sufficient.

Figure 8 shows Malthouse Lane, but neither the malthouse there nor the larger one at Womack are marked on the tithe map. There are several buildings north of The Grange, on the other side of the road.

Coming southwards, a gentleman, Mark Monument, lives at the Croft and next door is Edward Annison, blacksmith and wheelwright, with workshops beside his house. Behind there is the first Methodist chapel and George Smith and Edward Knights are living in Garden cottage.

hour of Eleven o'clock in the Forenoon.

Given under our hands this twenty-fourth day of September, one thousand, eight hundred, and thirty-eight.

JOHN BLAKE,
The Agent of WILLIAM BELLAIRS, Esq. Mr. JOHN TURNER, and Miss BERNEY.
JOHN SKIPPER,
The Agent of the Rev. ROBERT CHURCHMAN LONG, Clerk.
JAMES TURNER.
ROBERT MANN.

Commutation of Tithes.

WE the undersigned, being Tithe-owners or the duly authorised Agents of Tithe-owners, within the Parish of LUDHAM, in the county of Norfolk, whose Interest is not less than one-fourth part of the whole value of the Tithes of the said Parish, do, by this Notice in writing under our hands, call a Parochial Meeting of Land-owners and Tithe-owners within the limits of the said Parish, for the purpose of making an Agreement for the general Commutation of Tithes within the limits of the said Parish, pursuant to the provisions of an Act passed in the sixth and seventh years of the Reign of his late Majesty King William the Fourth, intituled "An Act for the Commutation of Tithes in England and Wales." And we do hereby also give Notice, that such Meeting will be held at the King's Arms Inn, in the said Parish, on Monday, the fifteenth day of October next, at the hour of Eleven in the Forenoon.

Given under our hands this eighteenth day of September, one thousand, eight hundred, and thirty eight.

J. KITSON,
Agent for the Lord Bishop of Norwich.
THOS. M. KEITH,
Agent for Joseph Sewell and John Blake, Lessees of the said Lord Bishop of Norwich.

ROBERT CARPENTER, Junr.
Surveyor of the said parish of Dunston.

Pursuant to the Act for the Relief of Insolvent Debtors in England.

The Court for Relief of Insolvent Debtors.

On the Second Day of October, 1838.

UPON the filing of the Petition and Schedule of WILLIAM GARDINER, formerly of Yarmouth, in the county of Norfolk, Innkeeper, and late of Colchester, in the county of Essex, Waiter at the Red Lion Inn, a Prisoner in the Gaol at Chelmsford, in the county of Essex:

It is ordered and appointed that the Matters of the said Petition and Schedule shall be heard by HENRY REVELL REYNOLDS, Esquire, or one other of Her Majesty's Commissioners for the Relief of Insolvent Debtors, proceeding on his Circuit, at the Court House at Chelmsford, in the said county, on the Thirtieth day of October instant, at the hour of Ten in the Morning precisely; of which all Creditors and Persons claiming to be Creditors of the said Insolvent for the sum of Five Pounds or more, shall have Notice by service of a Copy of this Order, made within such time and in such manner as is prescribed by the Rule of Court in that behalf. It is likewise ordered that the said Prisoner shall, within ten days after the issuing hereof, cause the Duplicate of the said Petition and Schedule, and all Books, Papers, and Writings relating thereto in his possession or power, to be lodged with the Clerk of the Peace, at his Office at Chelmsford, in the said county.

By the Court.

TAKE NOTICE.—1. If any Creditor intends to oppose the said Prisoner's discharge, Notice of such intention must be given to the said Prisoner in writing, three clear days before the day of hearing above mentioned, exclusive of Sunday, and exclusive both of the day of giving such notice and of the said day of hearing.

2. The Petition and Schedule will be produced by the proper Officer for inspection and examination at the Office of the Court in London, on Mondays, Wednesdays, and Fridays, between the hours of Ten and Four, on this Notice being exhibited; and Copies of the Petition and Schedule, or such part thereof as shall be required, will be provided by the proper Officer according to the Act 7 Geo. 4. c. 57. sec. 76.

N. B.—Entrance to the Office in Portugal Street, Lincoln's Inn Fields.

3. The Duplicate of the Petition and Schedule, and all books papers, and writings, filed therewith, will be produced by the said Clerk of the Peace, for inspection & examination at his Office above mentioned; and Copies of the Petition and Schedule, or such part thereof as shall be required, will be provided, according to the Act 7 Geo. 4. c. 57. sec. 77.

SHEARMAN & FREEMAN,
21, Bartlet's Buildings, Holborn, London,
For WICKS, Chelmsford.

The Court for Relief of Insolvent Debtors.

N. B.—See the Notice at the end of this Advertisement.

THE Matters of the Petition and Schedule of

Figure 7. From the Norfolk Chronicle & Norwich Gazette Saturday 6th October 1838. Price 4½d or 5s. 3d. a quarter.

Sarah Lucy and others are in a cottage and garden at the end of the old Back Lane. Opposite was a thatched barn (unfortunately burnt down in the 1950s) which belonged to Mary Anne Clarke at Albury House. She was a widow who farmed 13 acres and kept a butcher's shop in the house.

Opposite was the Town Farm, an old thatched house belonging to Royal Bond. The great barn next to it (the future site of the school) had just been pulled down according to the schedule. There were only four buildings down to the Pulk; (School Road) all probably housed two families. A little further out was Manship Farm with barns and 120 acres then farmed by Womack Bradford. The name presumably comes from a later farmer, Richard Manship, who would be there ten years afterwards.

Coming down the west side of the Street, William Garrett owned the corner house, then William Harmer "and others" the next two. (it often says "and others" on the schedule, so it is not possible to know all the people.) William England, the millwright, lived further along, next to another blacksmith, Charles Gibbs, and their workshops were behind. Robert Grapes had a house and yard nearer to the Kings Arms, which was kept by Edward Sandell and there was already a bowling green behind the inn.

On the East Side of the Street the farmer, Royal Garrett, lived in the big house, with his farmyard and stables beside it. Next door in the tall Georgian house was Charles Turner. Then came the grocer's shop kept by William Fendyke or Fendick. (150 years later, there is still a somewhat larger grocer's shop...) After that, on the corner, was the beer and bake house later called the Bakers Arms. (See Plate 20) owned by Royal Garrett and others. Going down the Yarmouth Road behind this, Charles Myhill and others lived in the house beside the road.

Opposite, Johanna Wells was in Rose Cottage. Various tenants and owners lived in the long row of thatched cottages, which make part of the charm of Ludham. Today they are well cared for. What a pity that the other handsome houses in the village did not survive. In the top cottage was Richard Stanton and somewhere in the middle was William Pigg, who was a pork butcher and had a pig farm of 3 acres over by the manor.

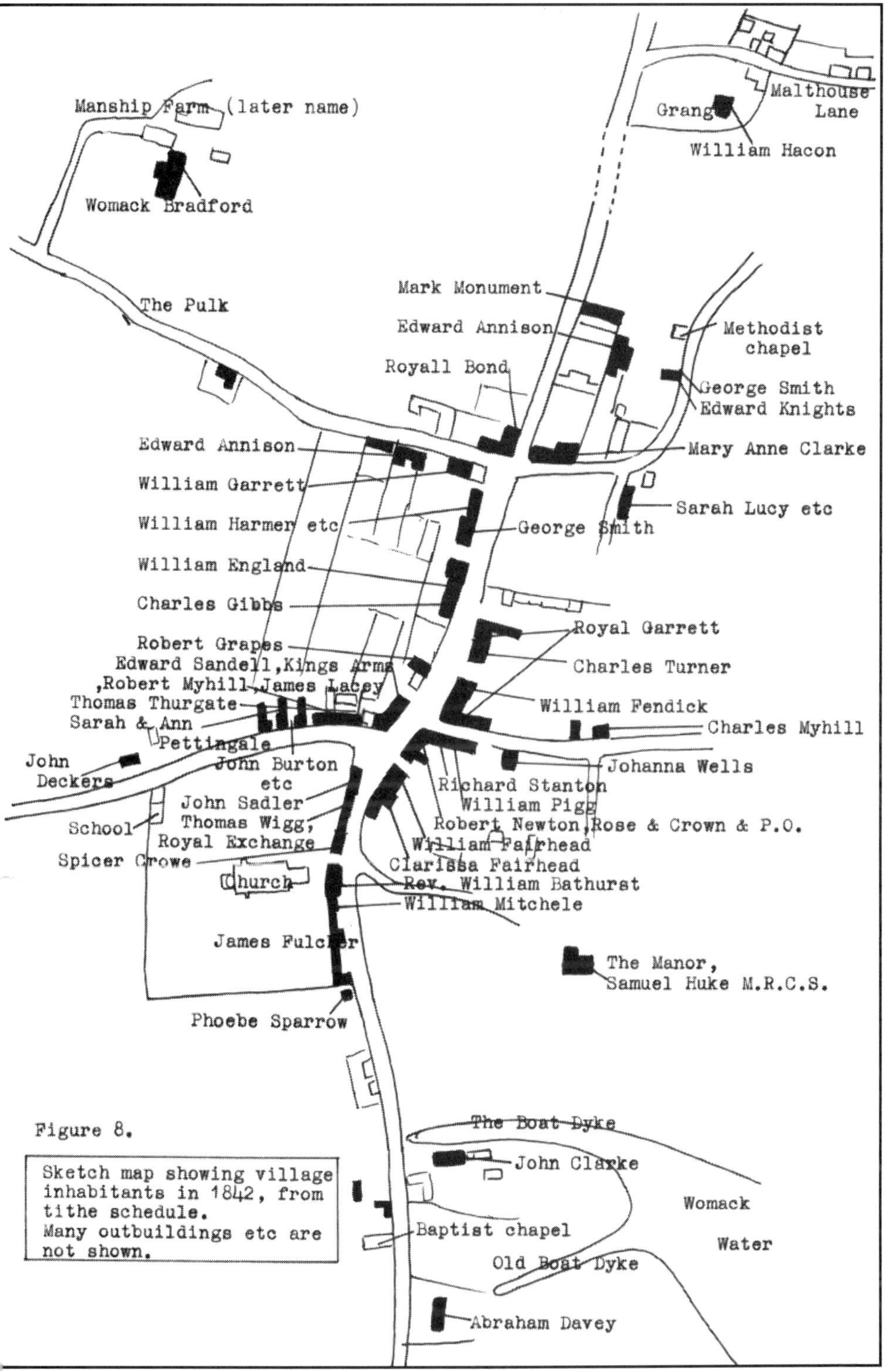

Figure 8.

Sketch map showing village inhabitants in 1842, from tithe schedule.
Many outbuildings etc are not shown.

Round the corner into Stocks Hill were the Rose and Crown public house and post office, kept by Robert Newton who was also the postmaster. Next, William Fairhead owned two houses and garden, (the present butcher's shop and next door). He was a carrier and made the journey to Norwich with his cart on Wednesdays and Saturdays. Later, he would go on Mondays as well. His daughter, Clarissa, kept a small general shop next door.

At the Manor were Samuel Taylor Huke and his family. He was a Member of the Royal College of Surgeons, the local doctor, and was also the medical officer at the Smallburgh workhouse. He was much loved for his kindness, especially to the poor.

Lower down, John Clarke was at Staithe House, by the Boat Dyke, or old staithe. (See front cover illustration. also Plate 60.) He was a merchant who dealt in corn, coal, beer, flour, oil etc. A customs and excise officer lived at Staithe house too; a certain amount of smuggling went on in the wherries! The boats came up to the road and were unloaded into the warehouse behind or straight into carts for transport. At the south end of the map was Abraham Davey at the thatched house there. (The Mowle). The Old Boat Dyke, a second inlet from Womack was then navigable almost up to his house.

Returning towards the centre, on the other side of the road, there were workshops and sheds opposite Staithe House, where James Fulcher, carpenter and wheelwright worked. Today, all have vanished. A little nearer the village, Phoebe Sparrow had a tiny cottage, also vanished. Then came the Town House Row, owned by James Fulcher. These six dwellings had once housed the village poor and had first been sold into private hands in 1790. William Michele and others lived next door to this, and next was the Rev. William Bathurst, vicar of Ludham, living in the temporary vicarage in Staithe Road (See Plate 49) which actually belonged to another cleric, the Rev. Thomas Tanqueray. Next, Spicer Crowe had a house and workshops, then another public house, The Royal Exchange, was kept by Thomas Wigg. (Sunnyside). On the corner, (today's Old Post Office) was the house and shop of John Sadler, ironmonger and druggist.

Going down the Norwich Road - then known by the much nicer name of Church Street - James Lacey was saddler and harness-maker in the first little shop and cottage. Then came others, including Robert Myhill and Thomas Thurgate, a third b1acksmith, with the forge behind the cottages. The last little cluster of rather fine houses contained, amongst others, John Burton and the sisters, Sarah and Ann Pettingale. Opposite here, in the corner of the churchyard, the National School had just been built the previous year, but the vicarage (the present day Old Vicarage) had not yet been built. The last house down Church Street (Lankester House) was occupied by John Deckers.

It is possible to tour the entire parish with the tithe map and find out the names and affairs of a large part of the inhabitants. It is interesting to see that of all the above-mentioned names of people in 1842, at least ten of those names were still in Ludham in 1942, and six are still there today.

One gets from the tithe map and its schedule a picture of the parish, at a time when there was a young queen on the throne, agriculture was still doing well, although there was still great poverty, especially amongst the labourers, and the population numbers were up to 924, almost the highest level before it began to decline twenty years later when depression began to set in.

Sources:
Ludham Tithe Map and Schedule, 1842. Now in the Norfolk Record Office.
W.E.Tate. The Parish Chest. Cambridge University Press.Reprinted 1960.
The second church register, 1685 - 1739, Now in the Norfolk Record Office.

Plate 18. The Saddler's shop and cottages in the early 1960's Photograph by kind permission of Eastern Counties Newspapers.

1842, The Saddler's Shop

In the rates book for 1842, James Lacey is listed as owning and occupying a house and shop. This was the thatched cottage just behind the Kings Arms and opposite Stocks Hill and the church. Lacey was a saddler and harness-maker by trade and he lived there with his wife Mary, their daughter Hannah, born in 1814 , a young apprentice and two lodgers.

In 1871 George Samuel Knights took over the property, where he was to remain for the next sixty-six years, working behind the bench until he died in 1937. There were seventeen children born in that small house to Sam Knights and his wife. One son, Albert, joined him in the business in 1919 after returning from the war. I just remember Sam Knights; he had a white beard and a kindly face. Albert, always known as "Knacker" Knights, died in 1968. With the decline of the farm horse he did little harness work, and his well-known shop was stocked with everything imaginable, from batteries and buttons to ground bait and horse brasses.

Saddlers and harness-makers always had the nickname of Knacker from an ancient Icelandic word 'Knakkr' meaning saddle. Today it is rather a name for horse slaughterers; in Lacey's time the two worked together, the saddler taking the horsehide from the slaughterer and dressing it himself. From this leather he made all the harness and gear needed for a working horse. Until the coming of tractors, there were three hundred or more heavy horses working on the farms around Ludham. He made the heavy collars and the saddles, of wood on a soft base, both lined with the traditional cloth, a blue and red checked wool and cotton flannel, and stuffed with straw. He made the bridles and all the traces and fitted the brass buckles.

The Saddler's cottage and the ones adjoining are built of brick with patches of flint and a flint plinth. They were probably built during the seventeenth century and were almost certainly five separate dwellings originally. There were five chimneys, five dormer windows and five front doors. I am not familiar with the adjoining cottages, but the shop and saddler's cottage had each a twisty caracole staircase originally. The downstairs windows were all small-paned sashes and only the saddler's cottage has the original one today. This used to have wooden shutters on the outside. It is not known when the end cottage was turned into a shop and the bay window inserted. It was probably as much for better light for the harness-maker's bench as for window display. Metal hooks on the wall outside displayed horse collars and harness. Four of the dormer windows were originally tiled and only one was thatched in a long sweep. Today, three are thatched and two are still tiled. The eastern chimney was removed recently. There was no fireplace underneath by then. It had presumably been removed early this century, together with the staircase that end. Mrs N. Hunt, a grand-daughter of Sam Knights, remembered as a child that there were two staircases and a lovely smell of new leather from the harnesses.

The large stone just beside the shop door was originally across the road, at the angle of the churchyard wall and served as a mounting block. It was moved when the wall was set back. It is a glacial erratic.

Sources :
Rates book, 1842.
Mrs N.Hunt, grand-daughter of G.S.Knights. 1975.
George Ewart Evans, "The Horse in the Furrow", 1960, Faber and Faber.

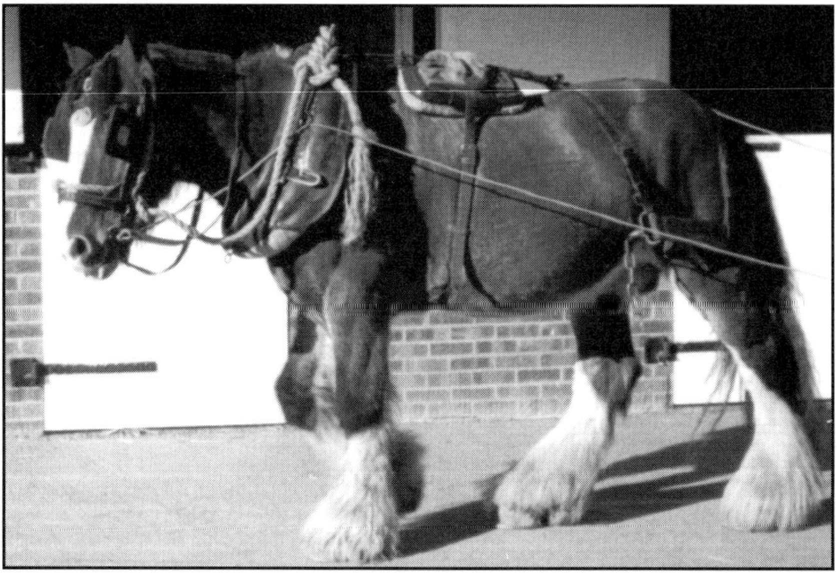

Plate 19. Farm horse wearing collar and harness, ready for work. Photograph by the author at West Runton Shire Horse Centre, 1995.

The Poor of the Parish

In the church chest were many papers of the eighteenth and nineteenth centuries regarding the poor. There were examinations, removal orders, settlement certificates, notices concerning bastards, indentures and some assorted correspondence.

In the early nineteenth century there was depression everywhere. The price of wheat and other commodities was high because of the Napoleonic wars and the harvests of 1816 and 1817 were a complete failure because of wet weather. Potatoes and tea were the usual food of the poor. Poaching was severely punished, sometimes by transportation to Australia. Many cottages were pulled down at this time by landowners, to avoid paying poor rates. In 1801 there were 114 houses in Ludham, of which two were empty, and there were 151 families. Of course, most cottages were divided into two or three dwellings.

In 1785 Tunstead and Happing hundreds united for the support of their poor and at Smallburgh was built the workhouse for their joint use, known as the Smallburgh Union House of Industry or House of Correction. It was built of brick and was altered and enlarged in 1836, and it could hold about five hundred inmates. It was surrounded by 24 acres of arable land, which provided some of the work. There was a master, a chaplain, a medical officer, a matron and a schoolmistress.

In 1894 the Unions became the Rural Districts, which is why Ludham is in the Smallburgh Rural District today, and representatives from each parish sit on the council, as in former times they sat upon the Board of Directors and Guardians of the workhouse. The three Ludham men on the board in 1840 were the Rev. Bathurst, Royal Garrett, who lived in the Street and Thomas Slipper of Fritton House Farm. The board met on alternate Tuesdays at the workhouse and the Petty Sessions were held there on the other Tuesdays.

That they tried to look after the health of the poor is seen from the minute book entry for September 1840, when the board discussed the extension of the smallpox vaccination programme. They decided that the out-relief poor should go to be vaccinated at the medical officers' houses on one day a week and that it would cost one shilling and sixpence. In Ludham, that would have been at the Manor, where lived Samuel Taylor Huke M.R.C.S. When he died in 1887, it was said of him that he was greatly beloved for his kindness, especially to the poor.

As the name suggests, people had to work there; many skeins of hemp yarn were spun by the women and children, clothes were made for the inmates and men worked in the garden or were hired to farmers. Those who were idle or who spoiled their work were punished, either by solitary confinement or by being deprived of their hot dinners and beer. Several absconded and usually threw their clothes back over the wall when they did so! The Guardians were especially indignant when anyone ran off with their "board cloathes".

In the church chest were half yearly accounts from the workhouse for Ludham parish, for between 1848 and 1856. The account of 1848 is as follows:

Parochial Statement of Account for half year ending 29 September 1848.
Tunstead and Happing Union **Ludham Parish.**

Dr.	£	s	d
In-maintenance	57	4	11
Out-relief	82	9	0
Maintenance of lunatics in Asylums	7	16	0
Extra medical fees or payments		10	6
Emigration expenses	-	-	-
Vaccination fees	1	17	6
Registration fees	1	6	6
County rates, first quarter	22	2	6
County rates, second quarter	15	19	7
Salaries of Officers & other common charges	52	17	11
Balance in favour of the Parish	122	12	4½
	364	16	9½

Cr.	£	s	d
Balance in favour of Parish brought forward	126	13	7½
Contributions & other monies paid to Treasurer of Union upon order of Guardians	225	0	0
Income from parish property	-	-	-
Credit, irremoveable poor charged to Common Fund	13	3	2
Balance against the parish	-	-	-
	364	16	9½

Happing and Tunstead Hundreds contained forty-one parishes with an income from the rate of about £4000 a year. In wintertime there were between three and four hundred poor in the workhouse, in summer, with the advent of seasonal jobs, this went down to between two and three hundred. The poor rate was basically a tax on property. Land-owners and farmers complained that a heavier burden fell upon them because of this. From one of the Ludham rate books dated April 1846, the assessment for relief of the poor of the parish was sixpence in the pound. This had to be collected by the over-seers, which wasn't easy as in periods of bad harvest or trade depression some small ratepayers found it difficult to pay and had to be excused by the justices. In some parishes the poor outnumbered the ratepayers.

There was also in the chest a list of 23 indoor-poor (resident in the workhouse) and 37 outdoor-poor (maintained in Ludham) with the amount in money or kind given to each person during the half year. The Smallburgh Union House of Industry was eventually demolished, but a good example of a local workhouse, now a private house, is still standing at Rollesby.

Parish officers first began to assume legal responsibility for relief of the poor in 1536, by an act of parliament for procuring alms from good Christian people, into alms boxes, every Sunday, holiday or festival day. An account book was to be kept in each parish and the collection of money, other than by the alms boxes, was made illegal. The large iron alms box in Ludham church dates from this time. It has four locks and its base is a tree trunk.

Many more acts dealing with all aspects of the poor and destitute were passed during the next three hundred years. The Poor Relief Act of 1601 ordered that the churchwardens and other householders of substance be nominated each year as overseers with the duty of maintaining the poor and setting them to work, the funds for this being provided by taxation of every inhabitant.... thus was born the poor rate.

Later came the laws of settlement and removal, which meant that any person trying to settle in a parish, or any parishioner likely to become a burden on the parish, had to prove his settlement there. The qualifications for this were: payment of rates on a property assessed at or over ten pounds a year, completing a full year as a hired servant, serving a full term as an apprentice or serving a parish office. In order to prove settlement, a person had to have an examination before two Justices of the Peace. If he could not prove it, a removal order followed to the parish in which he was judged to belong. There were 43 of these examinations in the chest, ranging in date from 1767 to 1858, and each one a little autobiography and full of human interest. These documents were very highly prized and a labourer's family would treasure for years any scrap of evidence that he had done anything to gain a settlement. For example, William Belson of Ludham was examined on June 23 1829;

"Who saith that he, this Examinant, at the Petty Sessions held at Martham in the said county, a little before old Michelmas, about twelve years ago, let himself as a servant in Husbandry from that Michelmas for a year to John Page of Ludham, farmer, at the wages of nine pounds and his board and lodging. That he entered upon, and duly performed his whole years service with Mr Page in Ludham aforesaid, and received all his wages for the same. That about two years after the expiration of his service with Mr Page (being then also a singleman), he agreed with William Womack of East Somerton, farmer, about three or four days before old Michelmas, to drive his team and with other Husbandry as he should be employed in, at the wages of eleven shillings a week and the living in a cottage belonging to Mr Womack, rent free, and to board in the House during Harvest, from that Michelmas until the Michelmas following. That he entered upon his last mentioned service pursuant to his agreement and continued therein until the Michelmas following and after that, two years longer, and received all his wages for the same That he was a singleman at the time and until about a fortnight after the commencement of his first years service, when he was lawfully married in the Parish Church of Potter Heigham to his present wife (late Mary Loades of Catfield, singlewoman) but he was not discharged previous to his marriage and after the same he continued his said service as above mentioned and has never done any act to gain a settlement since."

He signed his statement with a cross. But although William Belson considered himself to be "of Ludham" he was subsequently made the subject of a removal order in October of the same year, when the same Justices declared, on a printed form, that William and Mary his wife and Louisa, about 8 and Ann, about 6, their daughters, were become chargeable to the parish of Ludham, and not having gained a legal settlement there, were to be conveyed by the churchwardens and overseers to the parish of East Somerton, where the churchwardens and overseers of that parish were to receive and provide for them, and where, no doubt, a settlement certificate was issued to that effect.

Of the 27 examinations made, like that one, in the early 19th century, 13 of them concern farm labourers, the class most hit by the depression. There is one worstead weaver, a dying trade; one cordwainer, only the rich could afford his boots and shoes; one miller: two gardeners; three singlewomen; three widows. one deserted wife; a marsh drainage worker and a servant to an apothecary.

Here are some examples of the examinations. Only in the case of Elizabeth Smith in 1831 do we know for certain what happened to her, as there is also a removal order for her. Of the others it is sometimes possible to guess what the Justices must have decided.

Each is a précis in my own words.

1820 Robert Nursey, cordwainer, 54. Born Woodbastwick, where his father belonged. Was let at 13 or 14 to John Rushbrook, cordwainer, of Salhouse, for 6 years. After 2½ years, he was signed over to Thomas Ellis of Ludham, cordwainer, and finished his time with him. He kept his indenture in his pocket till it was chafed and worn to pieces. He thought Thomas was a certificated man from Woodbastwick to Ludham.

1825, James Miller, labourer, of Ludham. 15 years ago he let himself at the Ludham Petty Sessions held there, for 1 year to Edmund Pettingle, farmer of Ludham, at £77, board and lodging. He served Pettingle for 3 years. He has never let himself for a year, nor served a parish office, nor paid poor rates, nor had any estate of his own, nor rented £10 worth per year, nor done anything else to gain a settlement.

1826, William Pain, about 34, St Pauls, Norwich. Born Tuttington, father came from Walcot and died when he was 8, so he and two infant sisters spent 3 years in Smallburgh workhouse. Then he was let to Charles Earl of Ludham, surgeon and apothecary, as servant for 3 years. Moved to Cromer with Earl after 2 years. After a few weeks his master gave him his "time out". Lived with his mother at Tuttington, went into several services, then into the army for about 2 years. No act to gain settlement since.

1829, Edward Rice, aged 77, born Southrepps, where father belonged. 60 years ago, when single he was let to William Bately of Hasingham (?), farmer. 29 years ago he was employed by the Commissioners for enclosing and draining the waste lands etc. in Ludham. After the enclosure was completed, he was also employed by them to superintend the mills and other works of drainage at £15 per year and use and occupation of several runs of marsh-land, about 34 acres, and has continued this work and occupation of the land right up to the present time. Has also dwelt in a house belonging to the commissioners, rent free. That said dwelling was always of full value of £40 per year. It is not known whether Edward Rice obtained his settlement; there is another Edward Rice, also a marshman in 1851 who could be his son, but it may be just a coincidence.

1831, Elizabeth Smith of Ludham, single. Born Horning, where father belonged. In 1828, let herself to Mrs Ransome of Potter Heigham for a year at £5 per year. Then entered into a second year, but only worked till midsummer. Since when she has done no act to gain a settlement and is now pregnant and the child is likely to be born in bastardy in Ludham.

There is a removal order for Elizabeth Smith to be taken to Potter Heigham, also dated 1831. There were 39 removal orders and 25 settlement certificates in the church chest, representing a lot in terms of human misery and sadness. It is not difficult to visualise these poor people, with their few possessions, being bundled along by the parish constable in a waggon, or on foot if the distance was not far. Sometimes it was a very long way indeed, such as the removal order for Mary Neve and her two children, aged 6 and 2 from Yorkshire to Ludham. Also that of Ann Green and her two illegitimate children from Camberwell in London to Ludham. Her seventeen year old sister, Sarah, followed on another order three months later, suffering from a sickness which would produce permanent disability.

With regard to illness, there is a note attached to the removal order of one John Holmes from Yarmouth, addressed to the overseers of Ludham, saying, "if the man John Holmes is only ill from a temporary case they cannot remove the man, but if it be certified that his case is of a permanent nature they can remove, but you had better see the parties and inquire into it. If you find the man immovable you might give Yarmouth notice of the same".

The parish must have been involved in great expense with all the running about and letter writing concerned. It is very likely that this money, including appeals to magistrates and serving of warrants, would have more than maintained the paupers in the first place. But the unhappy poor were continually moved around, at the mercy of unscrupulous overseers or inhuman magistrates, although the parish was sometimes generous with payments of medical relief or clothing for the paupers. I should not have liked to be a churchwarden in those days!

Of the 20 removal orders concerning the 19th century, 14 were removed to Ludham and the rest to other places. Happisburgh, East Somerton, Witton, Potter Heigham and Intwood all in Norfolk, and one to Woolwich. No doubt there were a lot more than this, but presumably most people took their removal papers with them when they went, otherwise the overseers there would not accept them without proof. These orders were all printed forms, as were the settlement certificates, duly filled in and signed by the officials, whereas the examinations were on plain paper, just scraps sometimes.

One removal order to Ludham is that of Sarah Cooke, in 1858, singlewoman and Benjamin, aged 5 weeks, her illegitimate child. It is from Catfield, saying that she has never done any act to gain a settlement in her own right, nor her father who only recently went to live there, having lived all his life at Ludham and been employed and married there The father of the child is Benjamin Bell (or Orford) and also lives in Ludham. It ends;

"Therefore take notice, that unless notice of appeal be received within 21 days, the said paupers will be removed to your said parish of Ludham." This was carried out, as there is another document of the same date with orders to remove and carry her to Ludham.

Of the settlement certificates in the chest, all were of the 18th century, from 1704 to 1792, with the exception of two for 1862. On one, R. and E. Flatt with three children were to be settled in Catfield and Elizabeth Green, a widow, of 43 with one child, in Horning, on the other.

Other documents consisted of five notices to the constables to apprehend fathers of bastards and two others were orders for maintenance of bastards. In 1830, Harriet Weaver, single and mother of an illegitimate daughter had already been removed to Ludham from St Peter Mancroft, Norwich, when she was pregnant. The constables were to apprehend Francis Griffiths, labourer, late of Ludham. Perhaps he saw them coming. Of the maintenance orders, both were 18th century. In 1784 Sarah Palgrave had to pay sixpence a week and William Pye, thatcher of Ludham, one shilling, to support their daughter. There were three indentures, but these were not necessarily for paupers, being contracts for a young person to become an apprentice to a master or mistress, to learn a trade while working for him for a term of years. As the name implies, they were "indented" by being cut in half with a wavy edge and both parties kept half, which could be proved genuine by fitting it to the other half. In 1877 Walter William Lincoln was apprenticed to Eldred Webster of Martham to learn the trades of plumber, glazier and painter. His descendants are still in Ludham today.

Another indenture of 1775 concerns Sarah Wright of Ludham. Though it is not of the 19th century, it is worth including here as it shows how one may construct a whole life story of someone from local documents; this one from an indenture, a notice to the constables and three church registers. The indenture is for Sarah, "a poor child", who in 1775 is apprenticed to John Howse, farmer of Ludham, to learn the “art of husbandry business”. Mr Howse agreed with the churchwardens and overseers to teach and instruct the girl and also to "provide sufficient Meat, Drink, Apparel, Lodging, Washing and all other Things necessary and fit”. From a parish register it can be found that Sarah was born and baptised in Ludham in September 1762, making her thirteen years old when the indenture was made. It agrees that she will stay with Mr Howse until she is of the full age of twenty-one. Being apprenticed in Ludham and serving her time, she has gained her settlement there.

Unfortunately for Sarah, when she is twenty-four, in 1786, her name appears on another document in the parish. She has made a voluntary (she had not much choice..) examination upon oath before the Justices of the Peace, that she is expecting a child, and that the said child is likely to be born in bastardy and to be chargeable to the parish. She cites one James Bennet, late of Thurne, as the father, and the overseers have issued an order to the constables to apprehend him. There is no order for maintenance, so perhaps he was never found. Reference to the registers shows that Sarah, a pauper, had a son, Christopher, born in 1786, and another son, James, in 1790. But perhaps this sad little story of Sarah has a happy ending, for in 1793, she marries Robert Lane, also of Ludham.

There was a rise in illegitimate births at the beginning of the 19th century. Before enclosure became general the standard of living amongst the labourers was reasonable. Then, with the growth of the poor rate, landowners began to destroy cottages, so as to avoid paying so much, at the same time as the population was increasing. A young man found it difficult to get a home for himself and his intended bride, impossible to leave the parish because of the settlement laws and right out of the question to get a bit of land and set up as a small farmer. He had to live where he could, mostly in overcrowded conditions.

The Board of Agriculture Review for Norfolk of 1804 says on this subject that the changing ways of farming were having an effect on people; "a custom is coming in of allowing board wages to farm servants instead of the old way of feeding them in the house. This is one material cause of an increased neglect of the Sabbath and looseness of morals; they are free from the master's eye, sleep where and with whom they please and are rarely seen at church. A most pernicious practice".

The eternal problem of the poor was very serious and the

relationship between a parish and its poor was a very close and intimate one. In the days of parochial self government, the amount of time, money and attention spent upon matters relating to the poor seem to have been quite as great as that devoted to all other matters of local concern put together.

Sources:
W.E. Tate. The Parish Chest. Cambridge University Press, 1960.
Michael E. Rose. The English Poor Law. David & Charles. 1971.
David & Charles reprint, General View of the Agriculture of the county of Norfolk, Arthur Young, 1804.
Documents then in the church chest, now in Norfolk Record Office.

The Ludham Poors' Land Trust

This is a look at the Poors' Land Trust from its origins to the present day, and not just during the nineteenth century, although its income and advantages to the poor must have been more necessary than ever during that time. We have seen in the article on the poor of the parish some of the causes of poverty and misery of the farm labourer. At least one sixth of Ludham inhabitants were labourers and many others were also dependent on agriculture for their living.

The Trust was first established in 1630 when Francis and Phillippa Haddon left land in their wills to the town of Ludham. This was followed by more gifts of land during 1652 from Francis Jordan, Robert Gostling, Thomas Littlewood, William Green and Edward Townshend. The rents and profits from all these lands were to "Employ, Pay, and Distribute towards the Reparation of the Church and Relief of Poor People". Sometime during the next fifty years, three more pieces of land were added. All the land was in the west centre of the parish, around Laurels Farm and Clint Street, (see Fig.9) and are described in a Terrier of Town Lands, 1707, in the second church register. There was also a small income from the sale of the Town House, sold in 1790 and invested first in the Smallburgh Workhouse, and later in 1870, in government stock.

In 1802 at the enclosure there were changes. All the above agricultural land was awarded to other people and the comissioners awarded in exchange four pieces of marsh grazing and turf cutting land of a total of just over 138 acres. There is error in the commissioners' measurement of Gt Reedham marsh at How Hill; they give it as 185 acres, whereas it is only 85 acres. White's Directory for 1845 gives it more correctly as "about 80 acres". This land was given into the care of the Bishop and the Vicar, both of whom must always be trustees, and to the churchwardens and overseers of the poor and their successors for ever. They were required to let half the land, for any period not exceeding 14 years for the highest rent that they could get. This money was to be spent in purchasing fuel to be distributed among the poor inhabitants, who must be legally settled in the parish, and not occupying land or house of more than £5 yearly rateable value. The remaining half of the land to be used for cutting turf for fuel, this also to be distributed amongst the poor. The Terrier of 1707 stated that the distribution should always take place each Easter Monday.

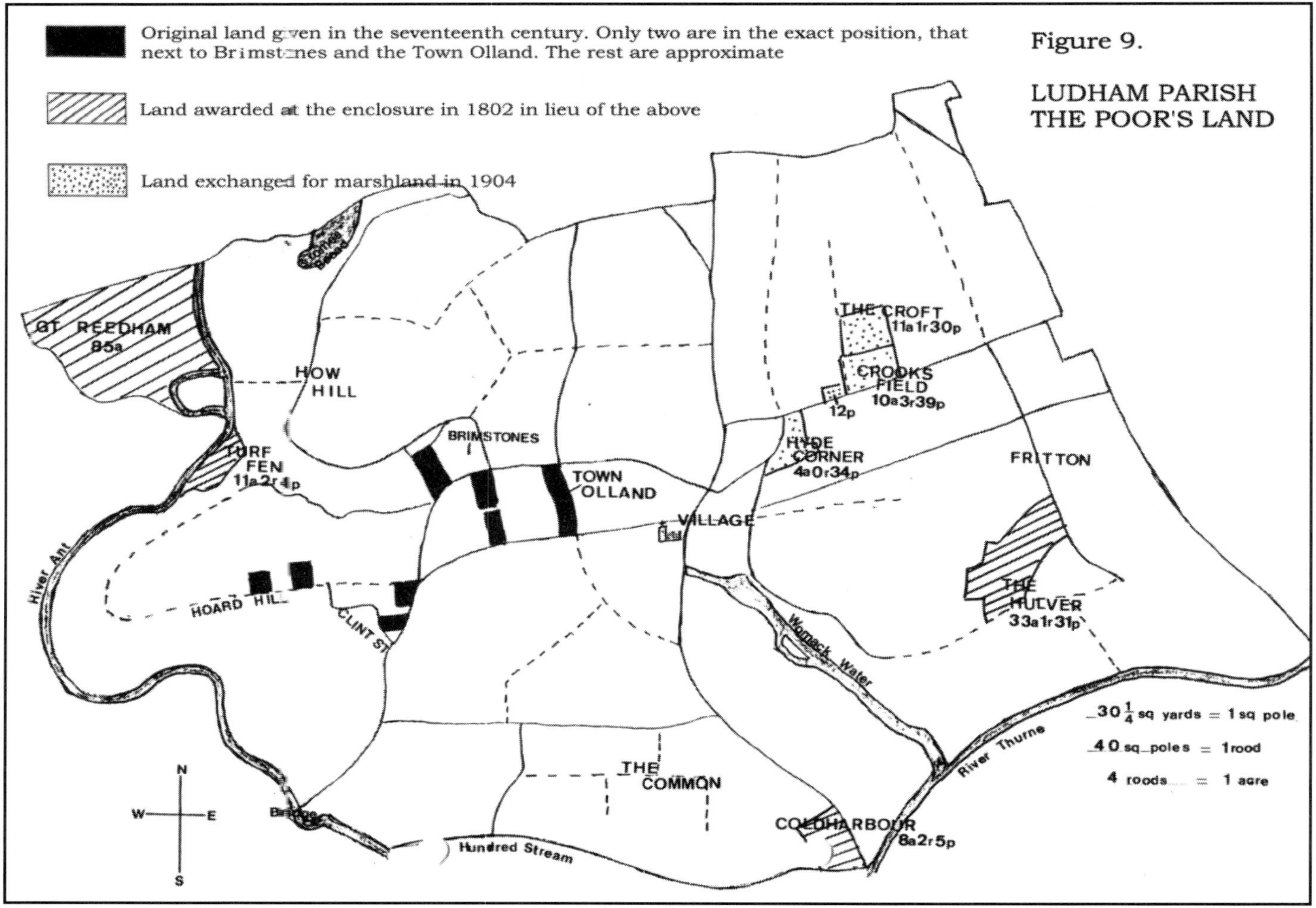
Figure 9.
LUDHAM PARISH
THE POOR'S LAND
Original land given in the seventeenth century. Only two are in the exact position, that next to Brimstones and the Town Olland. The rest are approximate
Land awarded at the enclosure in 1802 in lieu of the above
Land exchanged for marshland in 1904
GT REEDHAM
85a
HOW
HILL
TURF
FEN
11a2r4p
BRIMSTONES
TOWN
OLLAND
HOARD HILL
CLINT ST
THE CROFT
11a1r30p
CROOKS
FIELD
10a3r39p
12p
HYDE
CORNER
4a0r34p
VILLAGE
FRITTON
THE
HULVER
33a1r31p
Womack Water
THE
COMMON
COLDHARBOUR
8a2r5p
Hundred Stream
River Ant
River Thurne
Bridge
N
W
E
S
30 1/4 sq yards = 1 sq pole
40 sq poles = 1 rood
4 roods = 1 acre

The enclosure commissioners do not mention payment for repairs of the church, but this always continued to be paid up to the present time, known as the Ecclesiastical portion, and the Eleemosynary Portion was for the poor.

In 1904, the then Trustees, the Rev. Willmott, C. Blaxell, J. Kittle, H. Morgan, J. Gordon and E. England, met to discuss another change of land. Edward Boardman was building his new house at How Hill and wanted to include Gt Reedham and Turf Fen in his property. He offered to exchange these marshes, which had become waterlogged and useless for pastureage by about 1860, for four pieces of agricultural land nearer the village. This was a little over 26 acres, a lot smaller than the marsh acreage, but the income was much better, being £42 per annum instead of £16.5.0. The Charity Commissioners gave their consent and the deal went ahead. Thirty-seven years later, most of this land was to disappear under the wartime aerodrome. In March 1952 the Air Ministry finally paid the purchase price of £2,250 plus eleven years compensation money of £50 per annum, which made it £3,702.12.4. to be invested in the usual government stocks and the income paid to the Ludham Trust.

I became secretary to the Trustees in 1954 and two years later the Hulver, another piece of Poors' Land was sold to Clifford Kittle, whose farm it adjoined, for £525. There had been a long history of trouble with tenants of the Hulver, mostly for not cleaning out the dykes. It would have cost the Trust far more than the rent of £15 a year to do it, so finally, the Trustees were glad to find somconc to takc it off their hands.

Today the poorer inhabitants do not need turves for fuel or to pasture their cow or geese and almost all of the income comes from government stocks and insures a regular and trouble-free income. I see that the Trust has changed its name in recent years to a more politically correct one, leaving out the word poor. If there really are no more poor people in Ludham, then perhaps all the income should go to the repair of the church, as the original donors intended for half of it. Perhaps it is time for yet another change?

Sources:
Terrier of Town Lands 1707.
Enclosure Award 1802.
Poors ' Land Trust minute book.

Ludham Fair

The pleasure fair at Ludham continued to be held every year throughout the nineteenth century, nine weeks after Easter, on the Thursday and Friday after Trinity Sunday.

White's and Kelly's directories both refer to it, saying that it was originally both a market and a fair. This was obtained for Ludham by Bishop Redman during the reign of Queen Elizabeth at the very end of the sixteenth century. This was a much later grant of a market than most of the surrounding villages which had had markets since the thirteenth and fourteenth centuries.

Originally the fair and market would have been held on Stocks Hill and in The Street, both being quite wide spaces. Stocks* were always situated in a market place. The fair lasted well into the present century but by then it was usually in a field just outside the village. The market gradually came to an end as transport improved.

White's directory of 1845 also refers to a hiring fair held on old Michelmas day. This was for people in need of work who offered themselves for hire to prospective employers for the following year. Each carried a symbol of his or her trade or wore a traditional garment, such as a shepherd wearing a smock and carrying a crook, and a dairymaid with her apron and a pail. There must have been a very great influx of people into the centre of Ludham on that day; the farmers and other potential employers arriving by horse and trap, and those hoping for work trudging in on foot from the surrounding area.

* Stocks were a wooden board with holes for feet in which wrongdoers were imprisoned for a time, and the public would throw rotten eggs, or worse, at them.

Population and the 1851 Census

During the ninteenth century Ludham was the largest village in Happing Hundred. Only Hickling came anywhere near, with a population of 595 in 1801, rising to 823 in 1871, when Ludham was declining. Even Stalham, now considered as a small town, began that century with only 476 and did not reach a peak of 867 until 1891, which was probably due to the advent of the railway there.

The graph overleaf shows that Ludham began the century with 724 people, rising to a peak of 981 in 1851 and thereafter declining to 639 at the end. This rise and fall of population follows the fortunes of agriculture. In the eighteenth century, farming had made great progress and this continued until mid-nineteenth century and then began to decline. As we have seen, everyone in Ludham was dependant upon agriculture; if the farmers weren't prospering, then neither were the associated trades of miller, blacksmith, saddlers, wheelwrights etc., and if these weren't making money, then they weren't keeping the tailors, dressmakers, grocers or bricklayers in business either. Out of a total of 320 men of working age in 1851, 190 were in farming or an associated trade. Many women and children also worked part time on the land.

I obtained the complete set of 1851 census returns for Ludham from the London Record Office. They are fascinating to study and give one the impression of being among the people of that time and of knowing them all; their homes, their jobs and their families. This census gives details of the birthplace of each person, their age, occupation, marital status and their relationship to the head of the household. Like today, enumerators were chosen and on the given day, made the count, which then was on 7 April when they signed the certificate that they had truly and faithfully taken an account of the population and then delivered it to the Registrar. He satisfied himself that it was "as accurate as is possible" and signed it on 11 April, then passed it on to the Superintendent Registrar, who certified that "no inaccuracies had been discovered". They were all wrong - there is one inaccuracy, and the total population was 981 and not 982 as it has always been stated. I found this out by chance while analysing the returns; there was always one female short. The error - by the schoolmaster! is on

Figure 10. Graph of the Population of Ludham from 1801 to 1971. That of Wartime 1941 was an Estimation.

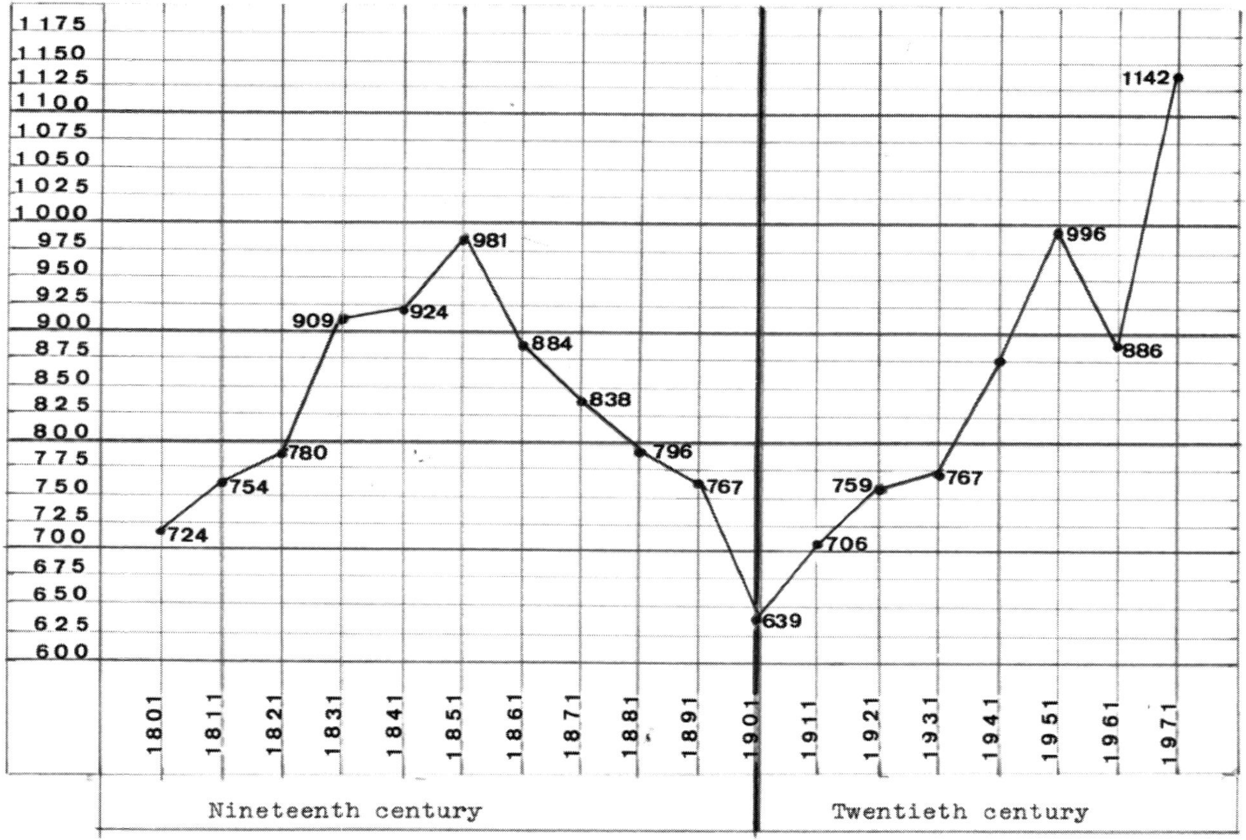

page 7 of the eastern side of the parish. The total is given of 11 females but there are only 10 on the page.

The enumerators were Hiram Coustos, 38, schoolmaster, and William Augustus Page, 24, farmer's son. Coustos's instructions were: "All that part of the parish of Ludham on the eastern side of Street, extending Northwards to Waltham (sic) Hall and Southwards to Cold Harbour, extending South-East to the Broad and Marshes to Jo Rice's and eastwardly to Fritton and the Yarmouth Road".

He begins with his own household in the centre of the village, at the top of the thatched row on the Yarmouth Road (today's gift shop). He goes east, down the road, listing 7 families and one empty house before turning into the Wennock (Womack). He found three households in the farm and the next house and 7 more down Horse Fen Road, which he calls Malthouse Road. At the end he walks round the marsh wall to the mill by the Thurne where John Rice lives. Then up the road through Fritton hamlet, via Green's Farm and 10 other families, and across the road to Slipper's Lane, where there are 2 more households before turning back after Thomas Slipper at Fritton Farm on the Heigham Road. He returns to the village over the Yarmouth Road hill, taking in the mill cottage, Hill Farm and another cottage. At Baker' s Corner there are 9 households and one empty house before the Bakers Arms itself. 7 families live along the east side of The Street, then he turns into Chapel Road (today's Malthouse Lane) by Mary Ann Clarke's house and finds an empty house and 9 families. Then 3 families on the Catfield Road and one down the old Malthouse Lane. Coustos next goes to Walton Hall, all on its own in the north, then back to the village, south from the Rose and Crown and down past the Boat Dyke with 8 households.

Then down to Hall Common, where 5 families lived in now vanished dwellings each side of the farm. Then right down to Coldharbour, counting 14 families, most of whose cottages have gone today. Then Coustos made his last call at the Manor, where he left his papers with Samuel Huke, the doctor, who was acting as Registrar for the census. They must have checked the figures together, but missed the error on page 7.

William Page's instructions were: " All that part of the parish of

Ludham on the western side of the Street, commencing North from Edw. Rice's, and extending Southwards to Mr Green's, including Ludham Hall, and Johnson's Street from the Bridge, to Mr. Jas. Garrett's, and the Irstead River on the West, and returning Northwards to How Hill".

Page dodges about a lot, but perhaps people were out at work and he had to return later. I imagine him on horseback. He begins at How Hill in the north-west corner, taking in Toad Hole at the riverside, where there were 9 people living in that tiny cottage. He just misses his own home going across to Turf Fen. From there he follows the river round, taking in 3 vanished cottages. Then to Whitegate Farm (now The Limes) and down what he calls Bell's Street, where there were 11 households, now only one cottage. Then Johnson's Street, the Dog Inn and Bridge House, which must be the little flint dwelling in Plate 4. Page went next to Ludham Hall where 3 families then lived. The adjoining cottages may be seen in Plate 22. Then in the street by Hall Common, he lists 6 households. This must be from Manor Farm up to the Boat Dyke, as Coustos had done all the houses on the east side there. Then Page gets to the street near the Staithe where there are 2 families. Then into the village, with 15 households, including the vicar's. He calls on 9 families in Church Street, then pops home to Pages Farm (lunchtime?) where he marks his parents' household before returning to Church street for 2 more houses. Then to the Kings Arms, then 4 more back in Church Street before tackling the west side of the main Street, where he does 10 households. Then to Manships Road where there are 7 families, back to the street for one he missed, then to Manships Road again for his last call, before taking his papers to Samuel Huke to be checked and signed.

Unfortunately the enumerators do not mark as many place names as one would like, just the odd road name or area. The only dwellings named are Ludham Hall, Bridge House and Walton Hall. Even the Manor is just given as "in the village". So it is not easy to know exactly where everyone lived. A comparison with the tithe schedule of nine years before shows a lot of people's homes, but it must be remembered that the owner of a property does not necessarily live in it, whereas the census does show everybody at home.

Over half of the population, 559 people were born in Ludham itself (see Fig.11). Many others came from a cluster of parishes around Ludham; the nearest providing the most, 39 from Catfield, 27 from Potter Heigham and 25 from Horning. Obviously most young men had to do their courting on foot, and the fact that rivers formed two thirds of the parish boundary, made access to the adjoining parishes of Irstead and Thurne more difficult. 15 people were born in Suffolk and only 9 outside East Anglia, of which 2 were born overseas. Thomas Barry, a barber and widower of 71, living alone in the street, was born in Quebec, to which our schoolmaster has added "America"... The other is a young lady of 19, Hebe Hazard, whose birthplace is given as the Isle of Java, Batavia. Her widowed mother had married John Bayles and they lived over his grocery and drapery shop on Stocks Hill (present butcher's shop). Two years after this census, Hebe would marry William Page, the enumerator, in Ludham Church.

The census shows 215 households and 5 empty houses. The analysis on page 75 shows the number of children per family and other details. There were 52 babies of one year or less, all born in Ludham except two. Surprisingly, no woman gave her occupation as midwife. The schoolmaster marked all the children who were scholars, but Page did not, so it is impossible to count those who attended school. The Hacons at The Grange had a governess for their two eldest. Twenty-seven households had indoor servant girls, of which the bigger houses had two or three and William Heath at the Hall had four. Ten farmers still had farm "servants" living with the family, this old custom not having quite died out here.

Lists of trades and occupations, with peoples' ages, are given on pages 87, 88 and 89. Six women, all elderly except one, and four men labourers are paupers. There are two interesting pensioners; Sam Myhill, who lived near Hall Common, was a pensioner of only 54 of the East India Company. Down at Coldharbour, in a now vanished cottage, lived Charles Belsey, a Chelsea Pensioner of 66 with his deaf wife whose place of birth was "not stated". Perhaps she did not hear the question.

Two trades are unusual. John Bowman, a widower of 85, was a mat maker. Did he make rush mats? Royal Bond, who lived at the end of the Street, was a Kiddier. This is someone who buys up hens, eggs, piglets etc., at farms and rears them himself. Kiddier derives from the word 'cadger', an itinerant trader.

Four shops are mentioned in the census. William Fendick, now 40, whom we saw in the tithe schedule, still had his grocery and drapery shop on the future site of the supermarket. John Bayles also had a grocers and drapers where the present butcher's shop is. Next door to him, 35 year old Clarissa Fairhead still keeps her little general store (see Plate 62). In the street, William Gaum is an ironmonger and druggist who has replaced John Sadler, who is now retired at 60 from his similar shop by the church gate, where we saw him in 1842. Down at Staithe House, John Clarke was still a merchant for corn, coal and beer, and Robert Newton, 53, was still landlord and postmaster at the Rose and Crown.

Ten years later, at the next census in 1861, the population had dropped by nearly a hundred to 884, then it went steadily down until it reached the lowest point of 639 people in 1901. Agriculture declined in the 1870s with competition from low-cost producers overseas. The railways had opened up the vast corn lands of Canada and the U.S.A. and wheat prices dropped from 55 shillings a quarter in the 1870s to 28 shillings in the 1890s. Ludham, being mainly arable land, suffered with the rest and quite a few people emigrated.

But in mid-century, when this census was taken, Ludham was a prosperous community with thriving farms, tradesmen and shops, and a healthy birthrate.

Sources:
The 1851 Census Returns from the London Record Office.
Raymond Page B.A., his History of the Page Family of Ludham and Oby, the Senior Line, 1765-1983, deposited in the Local History Dept. , Norwich Central Library, 1985.

I am grateful to Beulah Gowing for finding the word, 'kiddier' for me in the Rev. Forby's Norfolk Vocabulary, 1830.

Analysis of 1851 Census Returns

Males		Females	
Aged 71 and over	22	Aged 71 and over	15
Aged 61 - 70	22	Aged 61 - 70	31
Aged 51 - 60	34	Aged 51 - 60	27
Aged 41 - 50	45	Aged 41 - 50	35
Aged 31 - 40	47	Aged 31 - 40	55
Aged 21 - 30	81	Aged 21 - 30	90
Aged 11 - 20	91	Aged 11 - 20	98
Aged under 10	134	Aged under 10	154
Total males	476	Total females	505

Total population = 981. There is an error (page 7, east) in the original returns. They give 982 as total - 29 more females than males.

Married couples = 165.
There are 11 other married people whose spouse is absent.
People eligible for marriage, of between 17 - 40 = 154
Widowed, both sexes = 47
Total children under 10 = 288
Of which babies of under 1 year = 52 (26 each boys & girls)
Blind, one boy of 12
Deaf, one man of 45 and three women of 56, 53 and 75
Total born in Ludham = 559
Total born elsewhere = 418
Number of houses = 215 of which 5 are empty
Number of children per family:-
47 families had 1 child,
28 families had 2 children,
27 families had 3 children,
18 families had 4 children,
14 families had 5 children,
7 families had 6 children,
7 families had 7 children,
1 family had 8 children,
1 family had 9 children.
There were 11 visitors and 33 lodgers.
18 people had grandchildren living with them.

Figure 11. Birthplaces of Ludham Inhabitants from the 1851 Census.

Ludham 559
Catfield 39
Potter Heigham 27
Horning 25
Hickling 22
Neatishead 16
Norwich 15
Martham 13
Stalham 13
Smallburgh 12
Hoveton 9
Thurne 9
Wroxham 8
Burgh 8
Yarmouth 7
Sutton 7
Somerton 5
Salhouse 5
Repps 5
N.Walsham 5
Lessingham with
    Hempstead 5
Newton Flotman 4
East Ruston 4
Tunstead 4
Happisburgh 4
Barton Turf 4
Haddiscoe 4
Ingham 3
Irstead 3
Runham 3
Coltishall 3
Wymondham 3
Horstead 3
Rollesby 3
Hindolveston 3
Blofield 2
Eaton 2
Aylsham 2
Woodbastwick 2
Ormesby 2
Wood Norton 2
Belaugh 2
Halvergate 2
Corpusty 2
Sco Ruston 2
Hemsby 2
Stokesby 2

Total Population
of Ludham = 981

East Norfolk

Showing parishes where two or more Ludham inhabitants were born.

In 67 other Norfolk parishes, one Ludham person was born.

Fifteen people were born in Suffolk, most not far from the border with Norfolk.

Outside East Anglia, one person was born in each of the following:

Sheffield.	Bolton, Lancs.
Liverpool.	
Boston, Lincs.	Marylebone, Middx.
Langton, Lincs.	Bishop's Stortford.

Two were born abroad; one in Quebec and one in Java.

Three birthplaces are not stated and one is uncertain of her birthplace.

1851 Census : Men in Agriculture, Ages given.

Farmers (21)	Age	Acreage	Labourers	Site
William Heath	38	590	15	The Hall
William S. Page	55	400	16	Page's Farm
Thomas Slipper	74	230	13	Fritton Farm
William Hacon	65	175	10 (Also maltster)	Grange Farm
Royal Garrett	66	172		House in street, land scattered.
Aaron Neave	28	164	5	Hall cottages
John Page	47	150		Hill Farm
James Garrett	41	147	8	Limes Farm
James Greenacre	75	120	4	Whitehouse Farm
Richard Manship	51	120	4	Manship's Farm
Ann Bond	41	116		Hall Common Farm
William Green	57	80	4	Green's Farm
Richard Slaughter	60	56		Crome's Farm
William Thaxter	60	33		Manor Farm ?
John Clarke	35	18	(Also merchant)	Staithe House
John Felstead	64	16		Palgraves, How Hill
Mary Anne Clarke	59	13	(Also butcher)	Albury House
Robert Harrison	60	12	1 (Also boat builder)	Fenside
Thomas Ford	58	9	(Also cordwainer)	Johnson's Street
Robert Rice	66	6		Rice Cottage
William Pigg	54	3	(Also pork butcher)	Manor grounds

==

Trades Associated with Agriculture:

127 Farm labours, of whom 11 are boys under 15 and 4 are paupers.
2 Farm bailiffs - 40. 60.
8 Millers - 29. 43. 17. 27. 43. 22. 19. boy 15.
2 Team men - 57. 44.
6 Wheelwrights - 35. 36. 49. 22. 26. apprentice 18.
1 Cattle dealer - 36
4 Maltsters - 64. 26. 65. 66.
6 Marshmen - 25. 27. 34. 50. 54. 60.
3 Veterinary surgeons - 50. 22. 19.
1 Harness maker - 41. apprentice 17.
1 Drover's boy - 17.
1 Mole & rat catcher - 32.
7 Blacksmiths - 75 rtd. 55. 30. 25. 47. 16. apprentice 15.

1851 Census Trades & Occupations. Men, Ages given

7 Brickmakers - 30. 30. 45. 49. 67. 14. 11 boy.
5 Bricklayers - 52. 33. 41. 4. 19 apprentice.
5 Tailors - 30. 37. 21. 55. 17.
4 Shoemakers - 68. 55. 24. 39 (employs 2)
4 Cordwainers - 58. 47. 62. 35.
4 Carpenters - 19. 30. 73. 66.
4 House proprietors - 71. 76. 66. 66. (there must be others)
4 Millwrights - 44. 28. 29. 21. apprentice.
4 Grooms - 33. 22. 33. 31 also gardener
3 Gardeners - 30. 76. 31 also groom.
3 Annuitants - 59. 81. 80.
Curate of Catfield - 30.
3 Boatmen - 27. 35. 44.
3 Grocers & Drapers - 40. 42. 18 apprentice.
3 Merchants - 35 coal & corn, 22. 23. both visitors
3 Innkeepers - 37. 53
Postmaster - 32 also carrier
2 Carriers - 26. 32 also innkeeper
2 Boatbuilders - 60. 30.
2 Thatchers - 60. 71.
2 G1overs - 23. 61 .
2 Contractors - 42. 15 assistant.
2 Road labourers - 71. 75.
2 Police - 31 superintendent. 28 officer.
2 Hawker - 26. Tinker - 54.
3 Painter, Plumber & glaziers - 37. 35. 52.
2 Druggist - 58 also ironmonger. 60 retired.
2 Pensioners - 54 E. India Co. 66 Chelsea.
Vicar of Ludham - 42.
Matt maker? 85
Kiddier? 36
2 Butcher's assistants - 61. 27.
Inland Revenue Officer - 33.
Baker & beer seller - 51.
Parish clerk - 70.
Fishmonger - 28.
Sailor - 20.
Surgeon - 49.
Barber - 71.
Chemist - 19.
Basket maker - 39.
Schoolmaster - 38.
Letter carrier - 13.
Watchmaker - 50.

Census Trades And Occupations, Women, 1851
Ages given

27 General servants -	8. 1O. 17. 17. 17. 18. 18. 18. 19. 19. 19. 20. 23. 23. 23. 23. 26. 26. 27. 28. 31. 31. 31. 36. 38. 61.
6 Housemaids -	17. 18. 18. 19. 2O. 33.
4 Nursemaids -	14. 17. 18. 27.
1 Cook -	30.
7 Housekeepers -	18. 25. 26. 28. 37. 38. 50.
14 Dressmakers -	17. 17. 19. 19. 21. 22. 23. 23. 23. 27. 31. 38. 39. 60.
2 Tailoress -	44. 44.
4 Dairymaids -	17. 20. 22. 25.
6 Paupers -	46. 66. 71. 72. 77. 77.
3 Annuitants -	66. 83. 90.
Market woman -	27.
Butcher -	59.
Glovemaker -	66.
Schoolmistress -	39.
Flour seller -	48.
Shopkeeper -	35.
Charwoman -	68.
Workwoman ? -	42.
Spinsters -	65. 78.
House proprieter -	85.

Christian Names - There are:

71 Sarahs and Sarah Anns.

40 Elizabeths and 36 Harriets.

Unusual names are - Arletta, Clarissa, Phebe, Hebe, Almyra, Elethea, Primera. Cordelia, 0ctavia, Magdelina.

Unusual men's names are - Woodbine, Burley, Jethro, Abiathar, Abner,

Wesley, Jabez, Nathan, Remah, Hiram, Elijah, Armine.

LUDHAM PARISH

Figure 12. Sketch map Showing situation of Farms in mid-Nineteenth Century with Acreage where known.

From the 1851 Census Returns.

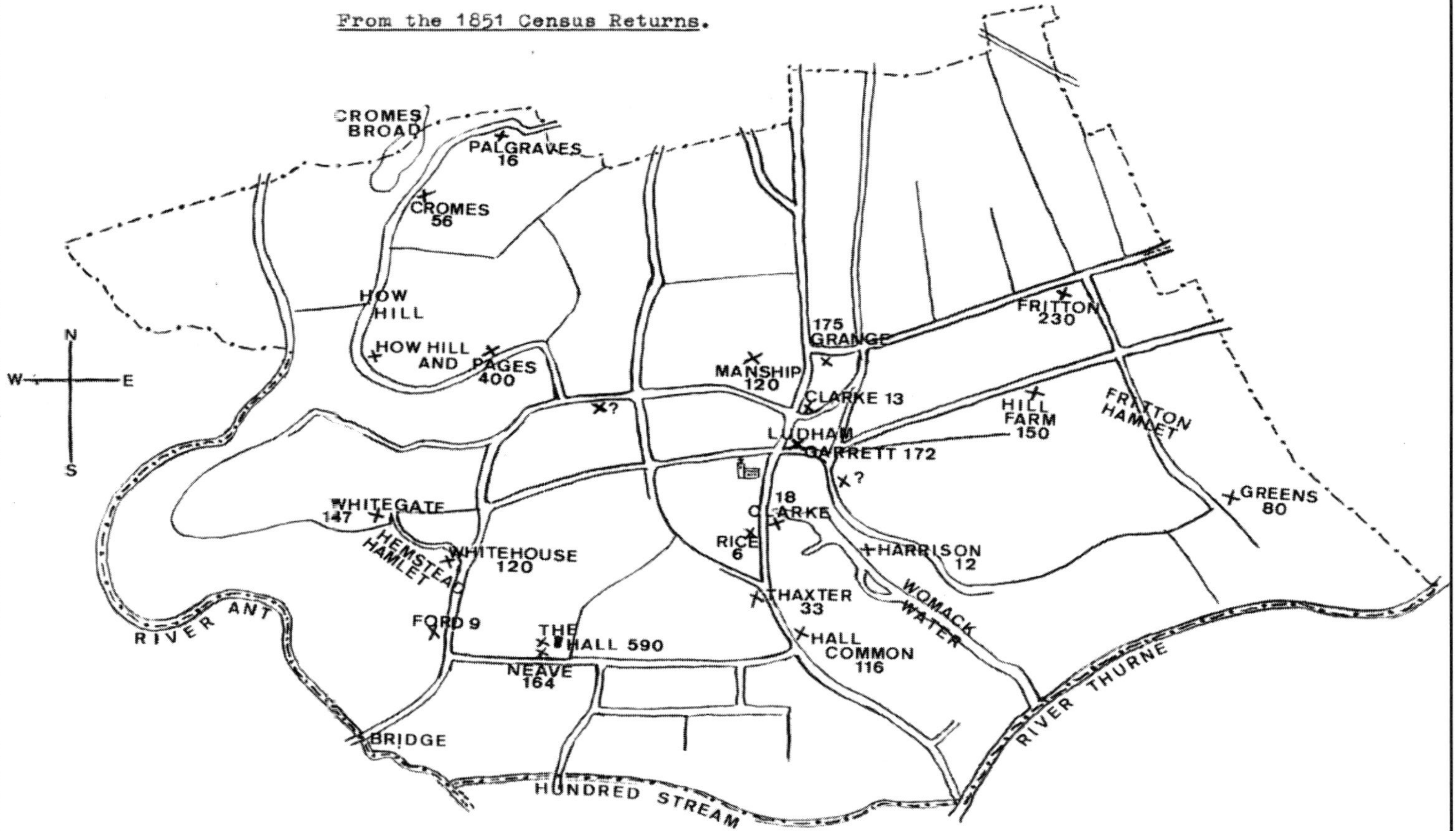

Notes on Some of the Older Houses

These notes mostly concern the exterior aspect of the houses and come entirely from my own observations, so there could be mistakes. A later facade can often conceal an older building.

There are many handsome houses in Ludham, but there is not space to deal with them all here. Four of the best ones were demolished about thirty years ago.

Demolished houses:-

Garrett's House *
High House *
The Baker's Arms
Tidmans

* Both in The Street, are fully dealt with in the next topic, "1857, Garrett's Farm Sale, page 107".

Existing houses:-

Ludham Hall
Dutch House
Hall Common Farm
Beeches Farm
Green Farm
Fritton Lodge
Walton Hall
Stone House
Pages Farm
Crown House
Albury House
The Manor
Cottage on Yarmouth Road
Hall Common cottages
Toad Hole

LUDHAM PARISH

Figure 13. Showing the older houses mentioned in this article.

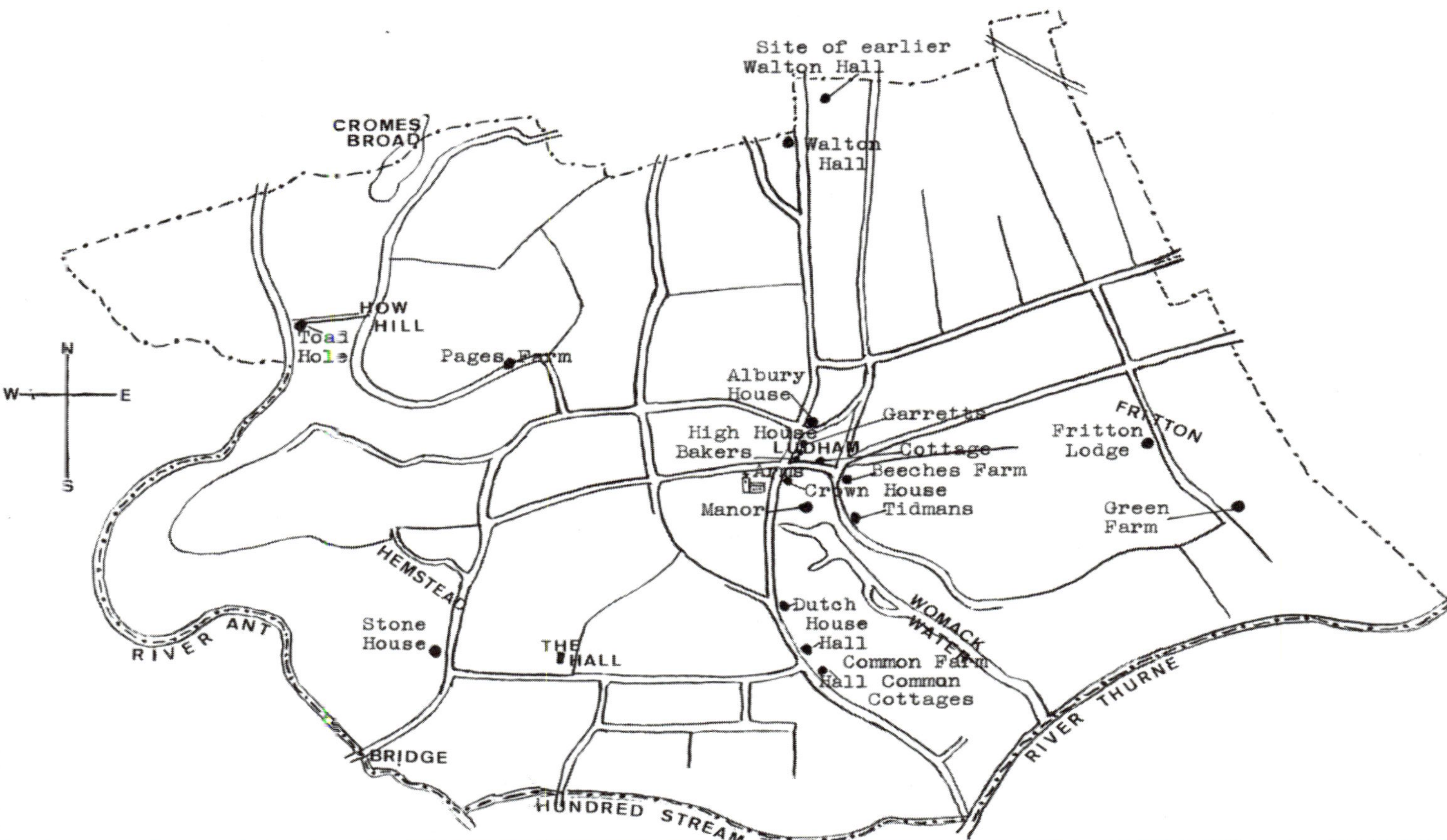

Plate 20 ***The Bakers Arms.***
Photographed April 1959.By kind permission of the Eastern Daily Press.

The Baker's Arms was a very pleasant building. Early eighteenth century perhaps, it was unusual in not having chimneys on the gable ends. That steep roof might once have been thatched. The dormer windows look like a later addition. Built of brick, plastered, it had a string course and pilasters at each angle and a deep tarred plinth. Three rings for attaching horses can be seen in the photograph. It was always a beer house with no spirit licence. There was a public bake-house at the rear, where people brought their bread and pies to be cooked, when not everyone had an oven in their house. It was demolished about 1959. One wonders why....

Plate 21a

Tidmans, Horse Fen Rd.

Photograph - the author, 1960's

Plate 21b

Tidmans, Horse Fen Rd

.

Photograph - the author, 1960's

So called because a local character, Emily Tidman, lived there with her father. A really lovely old house, it appears in one of Stanley J. Wearing's books, "Beautiful Norfolk Buildings".

Beside the malthouse near Womack, it is today replaced by a modern house. It was built of soft red brick in a somewhat erratic Flemish bond. There was a protruding wing at the front which contained the staircase. This had two small oval windows on each side, outlined in brick, which had at sometime been bricked up. A brick corbel was just above the top one on the east side, with no apparent reason for it. The top of the staircase gable and the central chimney had been rebuilt. It had a thatched roof and round finials on the gable ends. Various windows or doors had been bricked up or replaced over the years. A lower small house with a tiled roof was built on to the west end during the nineteenth century. The main house was probably seventeenth century. It was demolished during the 1960s. Such a pity.

Quite the most important building in the area is Ludham Hall. St Benet's Abbey on the marshes in Horning parish had its home farm on the nearest agricultural upland in Ludham. In 1536 after the exchange of land and property between Henry VIII and the then Abbot, this farm became the country estate of the Bishops of Norwich. The medieval house there and much else was destroyed by fire in August 1611, but a later building survived to become the present Ludham Hall. This had been built by Bishop Freake in 1580.

ate 22. ***Ludham Hall*** *- Photograph by Mrs H. Bunn c 1910. The cottages on the left were demolished soon afterwards. Note the 1810 facade and Bishop Samuel Harsnett's Chapel of 1627.*

Much information concerning the earlier history of Ludham Hall may be found in the books of the Rev. Anthony Harrison, 1563-1638, Rector of Catfield and Bishop Jegon's secretary at the time of the fire. He gives a long account of this, saying that it began in the brewhouse on a windy day and how almost everything was burned except for the Gentlemens' Lodgings (the present house) and not much else.

A later Bishop of Norwich, Samuel Harsnett, 1561-1631, spent a lot of time at the Hall and built the chapel there and the great barn in 1627. He was much beloved for his affability, eloquence and hospitality, and was a benefactor both to the parish and the church at Ludham. His chapel at the Hall was consecrated on Christmas day 1627 for divine service, matrimony and burial.

Plate 23. ***Ludham Hall*** *from the north-west. Photograph by Mrs H. Bunn circa 1910. Showing the house of 1580 with original windows blocked up. The chapel of 1627 has an earlier re-used gable wall behind the tower, no doubt the remains of a pre-fire building.*

The present house, built in 1580 was completely re-fronted in about 1810 with a plain brick front of six bays with a two bay pediment. The rear and gable walls are of flint and brick, with many blocked up original windows and doors.

The house inside is of post-medieval plan, with the original entrance and the original stairs beside the main chimney stack. The ground floor consisted of a hall, a parlour and a third room with a long wide passage at the rear.

The first floor was on the same plan and there were two attic floors, of which the upper one has gone today. Other chimney stacks have since been added. The cottages at the side were demolished after 1910 and a new cottage built at the south end at the rear.

Plate 24. *The Great barn at the Hall - Built in 1627. Photograph, the author.*

After Harsnett later Bishops did not spend much time at Ludham and the Hall was let to tenants from about 1674.

The first tenants were the Donne family and Anne Donne, who was born at the Hall in 1703, later became the mother of William Cowper, the poet. (1731-1800). John Johnson, born at the Hall on November 15 1769, was the son of Anne's niece Catherine, and it was Johnson who made a home for Cowper at East Dereham during Cowper's last years.

In recent years the Hall belonged to the Norwich Union. Now the wheel has come full circle after almost a thousand years, for in 1016 King Canute gave his royal estate at Ludham to St Benet's Abbey and now Ludham Hall and its farmlands have again become the property of The Crown Estates.

(With many thanks to David and Marian Ritchie.)

Sources:
The Rev. Anthony Harrison's books, Diocesan Archives,
Norfolk Record Office, DN/HAR 3/1, DN/HAR 4/1.
Ludham Hall, Norfolk, Joan M.Snelling, 1995,
Norfolk Studies Library, Norfolk Record Office.
St Benet's Abbey, Norfolk, Joan M. Snelling, 1971, revised by W.F. Edwards 1983. c/o Diocesan Offices, Norwich.

Plate 25. ***The Dutch House.*** *Photograph, the author.*

Once called Walnut Tree House, this is one of Ludham's oldest houses. The date 1603 is on the facade in widely spaced figures, somewhat hidden under plants.

This is a very early date for the Flemish bond brickwork in which the house is built. It is beautifully done with red stretcher bricks and blue headers. This bond was first used in England during the seventeenth century at a time when contact was frequent between East Anglia and the Low Countries.

There are also the "Dutch" gables with a wavy outline. These originated in Spain and came here by way of Holland just before 1600 and are found only in eastern England. William Thaxter farmed 33 acres from here in the middle of the nineteenth century.

Plate 26. ***Hall Common Farm.***
Photograph Broadland Photographics, 1967.

Very similar to the Dutch House nearby, but larger and later in date, it is brick built with Dutch gables and a thatched roof. There are spacious rooms inside and an elegant staircase. A large attic right across the top floor is reached by a hidden staircase in one corner.

On a protruding wing at the rear two terracotta tiles are inserted into the brickwork. One bears the heraldic badge of a Stafford knot, the other is hidden under vegetation.

Arthur Newton, born in 1886, remembered a terrible fire in the farm buildings here in 1894 or 95, caused by a spark from a threshing engine. It was attended by the manual fire engine from Stalham. The Bond family farmed here during the nineteenth century.

Plate 27. ***Beeches Farm*** *- north gable wall.*
Photograph, Broadland Photographics, 1967.

Near Old Mill Lane, this was once called Mill Farm. Seventeenth and eighteenth century, the older north gable wall is of flint, cobble and brick with at least one bricked up window.

There are a nice range of farm buildings and barns. (See Plate 9)

These are dated 1745 and 1797 and the one beside the road is 1748. In one of the larger ones was the threshing mill, worked by horses turning in a circle. The Greens, maltsters and brickmakers, lived here during the nineteenth century.

Plate 28a. ***Green Farm,*** *Fritton. Photograph, the author.*

Known earlier as Bounds Farm, this was farmed by William Green in the early part of the nineteenth century, which presumably accounts for the name. Like many local houses, one gable wall is much earlier, the east one being of flint up to the start of the roof, above which, the brickwork is very eroded. The west gable (right) is interesting also. Here is a clear earlier roof line on to which has later been built the attic storey.

A large window has been bricked up below the attic window and another window (or a door?) beneath that. There are traces of an earlier lean-to at the left. Both the older and newer roof lines have "tumbled" bricks, which usually indicates eighteenth century work. That being a time of agricultural prosperity, no doubt the farmer was able to afford to enlarge his house.

Note: "Tumbled" bricks are those inserted diagonally at the gable edge, sometimes just a few, here all the edge is tumbled.

Plate 28b. West Gable wall of the Green Farm, Fritton. Photograph, the author.

Plate 29. ***Fritton Lodge***
Photograph, the author, 1960's.

Also in Fritton hamlet, this house will be hard to recognise today from the earlier photograph. A large, probably early eighteenth century house, it was austere in its simplicity.

The smaller door was inserted in place of a window when it was at sometime made into two dwellings. There is "tumbling" amongst the gable brickwork and a faint pattern in blue bricks on the upper gable is cut by repairs to the chimney flue.

The long sweep of the roof down to the lower, later, chimney covered only a tiny lean-to at that end, the rest of the roof at the rear being the same height as at the front. Another lean-to had been added much later. Lean-to's served as a scullery in the old days and housed a large copper for heating water.

Plate 30. ***Walton Hall****, Photograph, the author.*

Standing alone in the north of the parish when it was first built, this house bears the name of a very much older vanished house whose site was just to the north-east. Nothing is known of the older house except that it gave its name to one of Ludham's three manors.

The name itself is interesting. Does it come from the old English name 'W(e)ald-tun', meaning homestead by a wood? Just nearby in Catfield was a very large wood. Arthur Young, in his Agricultural Review of 1804 says that it was 150 acres, belonged to the Earl of Abergavenny and was cut down in about 1794. Walton might also come from 'Wealas', the name given by Anglo-Saxon arrivals to the British original inhabitants. I am indebted to the late Dr. O. Schram for both these suggestions.

The present house is built in typical local style, but it is unusual in having four panels of flush flintwork with brick quoins and brick panels round the door and windows. The flints probably came from the ruined St Benet's Abbey. The bricks are very pale, almost white.

Plate 31. ***Stone House,*** *Photograph, the author.*

Stone House, once known as the Great House, is in Johnson Street. The facade and north wall are of regular knapped flint-work, which must have come from St Benet's Abbey. There are brick quoins and brick surrounds to the windows. Was there a date or initials in the space over the central window? There is a hipped roof and the main house is built of brick with several bricked up windows. The facade is a later addition to a much older house. Inside, on the upstairs landing is a very pretty Georgian shell-shaped closet in an alcove.

Stone House was once a farm and there were numerous buildings to the rear. William Clopton Johnson, who gave his name to Johnson St., farmed here at the end of the eighteenth century and beginning of the nineteenth. There is a reference in the churchwardens' account book in 1796 to Mr Johnson's "Mansion House". This is the house referred to in 1801 by schoolmaster Gabriel Smith when he certified that "a certain low room in the house of William C. Johnson, now used as a school-room, was to be set aside for the exercise of religious worship", for the Methodists.

Plate 32. ***Pages Farm.*** *Photograph, the author.*

On the way to How Hill, this was the home of the Page family. It differs from other houses in the parish in having a facade made up of two gables with a roof valley in the centre. It is brick built with low-pitched tiled roofs. There was a much older wall beside it, extending back among the farm buildings. In one of the rate books it is referred to as the "Old Hall" and in the churchwarden's account book of 1791 there is a reference to "Page's New House". Was this it?

The Page family was extensive, as may be seen from the church registers and the tombstones. They farmed in Ludham as well as in the Fleggs from the eighteenth century onwards.

William Sherwood Page, 1795-1876, who lived in this house, came to Ludham from Ormesby in 1818. His eldest son, Sherwood William, moved to How Hill Farm next door after his marriage and the two farms were worked as one.

The barn at Pages Farm is very similar both to the Great Barn at Ludham Hall and to another barn at nearby Sharpe Street, Catfield. The date of the barn at the Hall is known 1627.

All three barns are brick built with buttresses and a string course and a plinth and have square pierced brick ventilation openings. Page's barn has buttresses only at the angles and beside the door, the bays being marked by brick pilasters. The upper gable end has been filled with wood slats. It was presumably once thatched.

Surely, if there is an early seventeenth century barn here, there might have been a house of similar date, or earlier, beside it?

I am grateful to Raymond Page for information from his "History of the Page Family of Ludham and Oby, The Senior Line, 1765 - 1983" Local Studies Library, Norfolk Record Office.

'late 33. ***The Barn at Pages Farm.***
Photograph , Broadland Photographics Ltd.

Plate 34a.

The Manor

Plate 34b.

Rear of
The Manor

Photograph,
the author.

A thatched brick house, with a plain facade and rounded tops to the windows. Later porch. At the rear are two thatched wings, tall and narrow, with a more recent wing, with a lower pitched tiled roof, on the end of the west one.

One has the impression that there was a much older house beneath all this and there is some stonework inside.

During the nineteenth century this was the home of Samuel Taylor Huke M.R.C.S., local doctor and surgeon and medical officer for the Smallburgh House of Industry for over 50 years.

Plate 35. ***Crown House,*** *Photograph, the author.*

In the village centre is Crown House, which was the Rose and Crown public house from at least 1752. Also the Post Office for 33 years when Robert Newton was both postmaster and publican during the nineteenth century.

Plate 36. ***Albury House,*** *Photograph, the author.*

At the north end of the Village Street, it has a hipped roof with lions' heads around the cornice. The 1946 photograph shows it with the original front door and fanlight and double arch.

Down the side lane, the dark window was the door to Mary Ann Clarke's butcher's shop during the nineteenth century. Inside was an ingenious arrangement of little windows, which enabled Mary Ann to see from either her kitchen or front room when a customer entered her shop. In 1851 Mary Ann was a widow of 59, running the shop and farming 13 acres with the help of her son. There were farm buildings behind and a large thatched barn, unfortunately destroyed by fire in the early 1950s.

During the 1960s Albury House was greatly altered inside, the older part at the rear demolished and the front door replaced.

Mrs Clarke's daughter, Emily, who lived here with her mother, died in 1904 and left a substantial amount of money, part of which became the Emily Clarke Trust, for the repair of the church and the churchyard walls and also for providing clothes, coal and blankets to the poor of Ludham.

The houses just described are all buildings of a certain size and standing, built and lived in by comparatively wealthy inhabitants of Ludham. What of the farm labourers? Many of the smaller, humbler dwellings seen on the enclosure and tithe maps of 1802 and 1842 have vanished; some pulled down long ago to avoid paying rates when agriculture slumped during the nineteenth century.

The following three are good examples of the poorer peoples' cottages. -

Plate 37.

Cottage on the Yarmouth Road just outside the village.

This tiny cottage, with its thatched roof, would have been a typical nineteenth century farm labourer's cottage.

Photograph, the author, 1960's.

Plate 38.

Hall Common Cottages. *Nearly derelict in 1953.*

Photograph, E. A. Howes.

These cottages originally belonged to the Fleggburgh Hall Estate and were later sold to George Bond at Hall Common Farm. They were a row of three dwellings with the furthest one being older and smaller than the other two. This one had only two low rooms and no stairs. There must have been a ladder for access to the upper room. Here there was no dormer, only two tiny windows in the gable end. There was a large fireplace and no oven.

The other two dwellings were late eighteenth century, with two rooms downstairs and one room upstairs. All are on the 1802 enclosure map. There is "tumbling" of bricks on the gable seen from the road, above a slight corbel where the thatched roof begins. The rear chimneys look like later additions and they serve wall ovens, which must have been added later, together with Victorian fireplaces with hobs in the main rooms.

Outside there were three sheds, three privies and a flint and brick stable nearby. Water was obtained from a well with a lead pump near the road.

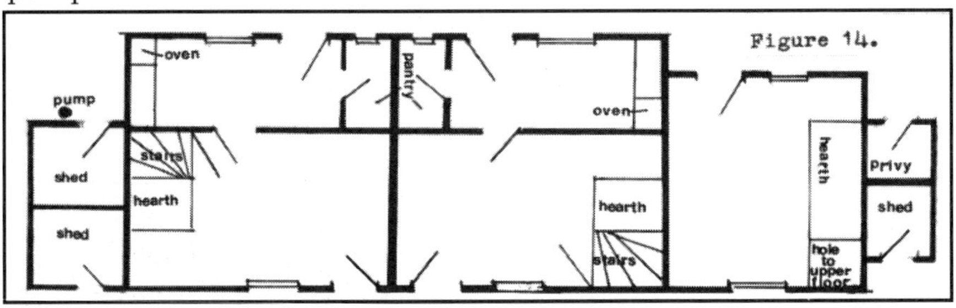

Figure 14. Sketch Plan of Hall Common Cottages Ground Floors, 1953 before alterations (not to scale)

Plate 39

The Older Cottage.

Photograph, E.A. Howes.

Plate 40.

From the Road.

Photograph,
E.A. Howes.

Hall Common Cottages, 1953

Plate 41.

The Wall Oven.

The fire for heating this was in a small hole beneath, where the iron is.

Photograph,
the author.

In about 1973, I was asked to give an illustrated talk at How Hill Educational centre to the Carnegie Trust on the subjects of Toad Hole and Cromes Broad. I understood that there was a possibility of a grant being given to make something of these.

My talk must have been successful as I have since visited the delightful little museum at Toad Hole.

Plate 42. ***Toad Hole, How Hill Staithe.***
Photograph, Clifford Mumby.

This little cottage is not marked on the enclosure map of 1802 and yet the "tumbling" of the brickwork just above the little corbels at the roof line and again just beneath the chimney, could indicate eighteenth century work. Could the gables be older than the other walls? It was a frequent practice in those times to re-use a good gable. The front wall brickwork is in a neat and smooth Flemish bond and the gables are in an irregular bond and are rough and eroded. The west apex has been renewed. A door has been bricked up on the south front.

This is a single dwelling, on a different plan from Hall Common cottages. The hearth and stairs arrangements are the same but across the other end of the main room are a good-sized pantry and storeroom. A brick lean-to has been added much later with a separate roof. Upstairs is divided into two bedrooms. On an angle of the brickwork near the outside door is a deep scar where someone had sharpened his knife every day.

In the 1842 tithe schedule it was owned by William Sherwood Page and occupied by John Cooke.

In the 1851 census, William Davey, a bricklayer, lived in this tiny house with six children, aged from 8 to 21, a grandson and a visiting child!

More recently, Curtiss, ferryman, eel and mole catcher, lived here. He ferried people across to Great Reedham marsh and to Irstead.

The Marshman's Museum here, run by the Broads Authority with the How Hill Trust, is well worth a visit.

Plate 43. **Toad Hole.** *Photograph, Clifford Mumby.*

NORFOLK.

Particulars and Conditions of Sale

OF

VALUABLE ESTATES

ALL FREEHOLD OR COPYHOLD FINE CERTAIN,

SITUATE

IN THE PARISH OF LUDHAM;

COMPRISING AN EXCELLENT

Farm-Residence & Agricultural Buildings,

DWELLING HOUSE,

SEVERAL COTTAGES AND TENEMENTS,

POST WINDMILL, WITH WAREHOUSE, STABLE, &c.

Numerous Inclosures of remarkably fine Arable, Pasture, and Marsh Land, containing together by survey

173A. 2R. 8P.

WHICH WILL BE SOLD BY AUCTION, BY

MESSRS. BUTCHER,

AT THE

KING'S ARMS INN, LUDHAM, NORFOLK,

ON FRIDAY, SEPTEMBER THE 11TH, 1857,

AT THREE O'CLOCK IN THE AFTERNOON,

IN SEVENTEEN LOTS.

J. FLETCHER, PRINTER, POTTERGATE STREET, NORWICH.

Figures 15a. & 15b.

'Particulars and Conditions of Sale'

James Garrett was Royal's brother and farmed what was then known as Whitegate Farm.

(Some of the words are missing below)

☞ **The Vendors reserve to themselves all the Hay and Manure now being or which shall be upon and about the several Lots at Michaelmas next, and to dispose of the same as they shall think proper.**

The purchaser of any Lot on which there shall be Turnips, Mangel Wurzel, or New Lays, is to pay for the same according to a valuation to be made thereof, at the joint and equal expense of the vendors and purchaser, by two indifferent persons, one to be chosen by each party, or pute between such two persons, then by an umpire to be chosen by them before they commence their valuation; and the purchaser of any Lot upon which Corn shall have been grown in the present year, is also to pay for the Threshing and Dressing such Corn, according to the prices paid in Ludham and the neighbourhood thereof, and shall carry out the Corn when threshed to any place not exceeding the distance of Yarmouth, being allowed the Straw, Chaff, and Colder arising therefrom; and if any difference or dispute shall arise as to the quantity of Corn grown upon any Lot, or as to the quantity of Straw, Chaff, and Colder arising therefrom, such dispute shall be referred to Mr. James Garrett, of Ludham, whose decision shall be conclusive between the parties interested.

The vendors reserve the right to the use of the Barns and Stackyards, part of Lot 1, for all usual purposes, until the 1st day of May, 1858.

1857, Garrett's Farm Sale

On Friday September 11th 1857 an important auction sale took place at the Kings Arms Inn at 3 o'clock in the afternoon. The sale was conducted by Messrs Butcher of Norwich and was in seventeen lots. It must have attracted a very large crowd to Ludham that day.

Mr Royal Garrett was selling his house and farm, including several dwellings, a post windmill and fine arable and pasture land, the total acreage of which was 173a 2r 8p. According to the sale particulars he was still living in his house at the time of the sale. He was about 72 and may have thought it was time to retire. But he had four sons, Jabez, 32, Abithar, 28, Nathan, 25, and Jethro, 21, three of whom were employed on the farm and the fourth a miller.

Garrett' s farm was unusual in that it was not a self-contained unit amid its fields. The house was in the very centre of Ludham Street and the land was in six different parts of the parish. That being so, it could not have been economic to run. (see figure 18)

Lot no. 1 consisted of Garrett's house, the adjoining farm buildings and a cottage and the field behind called Thorofare Piece, later known as Latchmoor and now built over with a modern estate. There was a "good Barn, Cart-horse Stable for Ten Horses with Hay-loft, three-stall Riding-horse Stable, Harness-house, Warehouse and Granary; Gig-house, Turnip-house, Bullock and Wagon Lodges and enclosed yards etc." Beside this was a well-planted orchard, and garden and a stackyard.

Just before demolition in the 1960s I prowled around the house, made a sketch plan and took photographs. It was a lovely house and could have been restored instead of demolished. The facade was eighteenth century, but the rear wall was earlier, being a neat pattern of brick, flint and cobbles, with blocked original windows upstairs.

Royal Garrett's House
Sketch plan, not to scale of the now demolished house on the East Side of Ludham Street

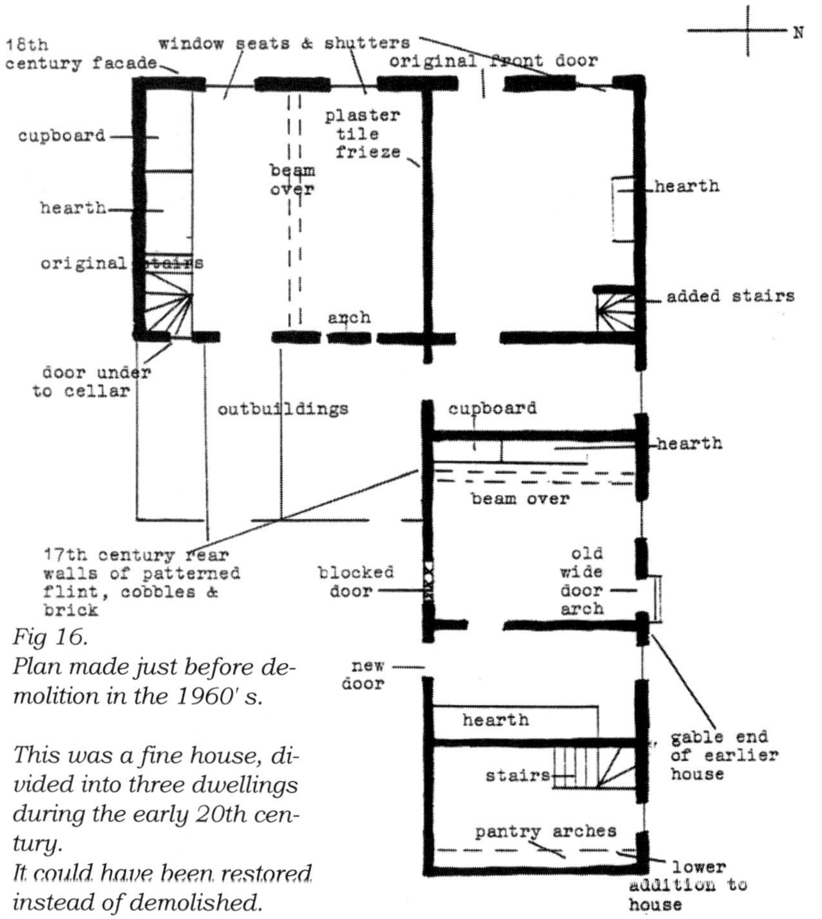

Fig 16.
Plan made just before demolition in the 1960' s.

This was a fine house, divided into three dwellings during the early 20th century.
It could have been restored instead of demolished.

Around the main front room was a frieze of 17th century moulded plaster tiles of three patterns; phoenix, griffon and eagle. Three are in the Bridewell Museum.
In the mid 19th century Royal Garrett, farmer of 172 acres, lived here with his wife, four sons, two farm servants, a dairymaid and a housemaid. A stackyard and stable range were on the north.

Joan M. Snelling

Sketch plan of the now demolished house on the East Side of Ludham Street (not to scale)

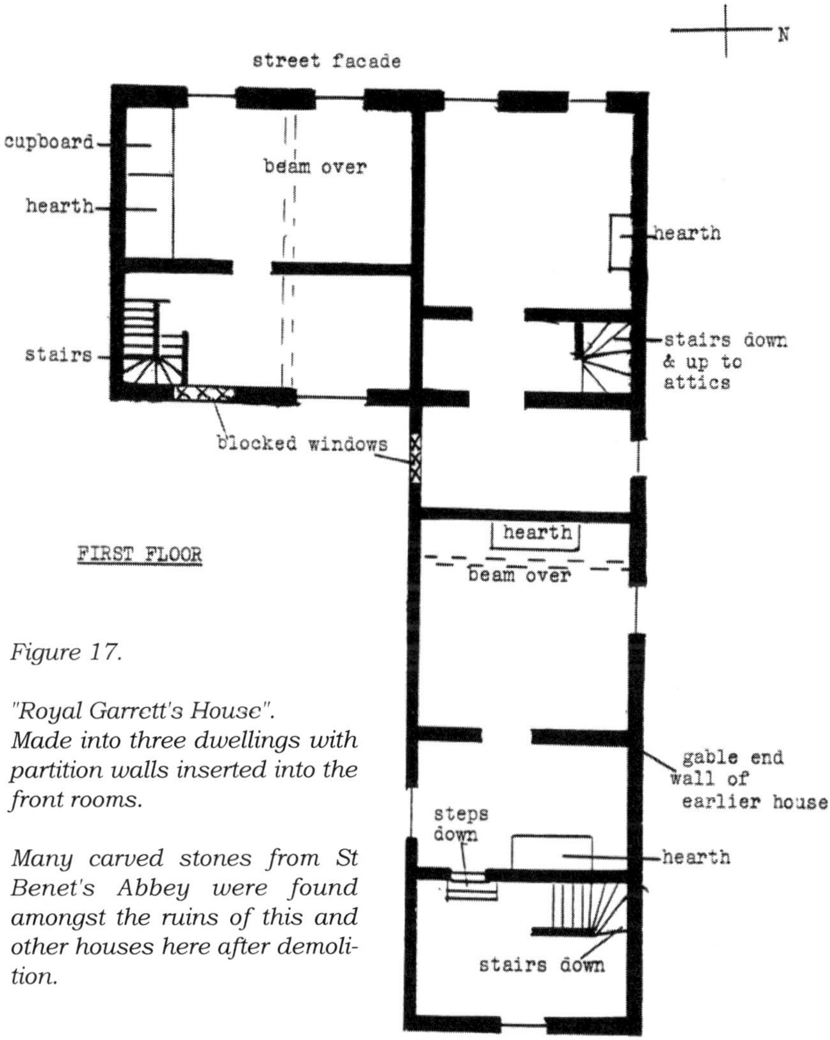

Figure 17.

"Royal Garrett's House". Made into three dwellings with partition walls inserted into the front rooms.

Many carved stones from St Benet's Abbey were found amongst the ruins of this and other houses here after demolition.

Joan M. Snelling

Plate 44. Garrett's house on the left. A downstairs window has been made into a door. Then the three storey house, (Lot 6 in the sale) which later became the police house, with a lock-up in the cellar. Next Thrower's shop with the Baker's Arms just visible behind - Old postcard c. 1930.

Plate 45. Rear of Garrett's house, rather cluttered with out buildings. Note brick, flint and cobble pattern and the blocked windows. Photograph, the author.

Plate 46. North side of Garrett's house. Note flint and cobble panel on original gable end. Photograph, the author.

Plate 47. Cottage on the end of vanished stable block, opposite the above north side of house. Photograph, the author.

The back wall of the rear wing had two panels of brick, flint and cobbles at the top, but up to the first floor the lower part of the wall was a hotchpotch of the same materials with one, possibly two, blocked original windows upstairs, (see photographs and plans).

There was no access on either floor to the rear wing, the house having been divided into three dwellings in recent times. It must have been one house in Garrett's time, the sale description being "3 Sitting Rooms, 2 Kitchens, storeroom, Pantry, 3 Cellars, 6 Bedrooms and 5 Attics". At the 1851 census there were 10 people living there; Royal and Hannah Garrett, their four sons, two farm servants, a housemaid and a dairymaid.

The cottage, also part of lot 1, was of brick and tile (plate 47) and adjoined the stable block. This was also demolished to build the modern houses, but the stable range was demolished long before. Lots 6, 7, 8 and 14 were all dwelling houses. The house next door to Garrett's was Lot 6. This was a handsome Georgian building of three stories. In 1857 it was shared by two families and there were seven "Sleeping Rooms". It unfortunately burned down during the 1950s when a young couple were about to restore it, and its ruins demolished with the rest. Lot 7 was a brick and thatch cottage with large yard, gardens and sheds, adjoining the Kings Arms Inn. Today this has gone, and would have stood on the site that became, earlier this century, Brook's original garage, looking down the Yarmouth Road.

Lot 8 was down Staithe Road and consisted of a brick and tile house adjoining the churchyard and divided into two dwellings, a brick and tile workshop, a tenement and a cottage, all adjoining. The four dwellings were all occupied by tenants. The house was Sunnyside and the rest were on the site of the row of garages or sheds that stretch from it to the side gate of the churchyard.

Lot 11 was interesting, being "a Post Windmill driving two pairs of Stones and in good working repair, with a Cottage or Warehouse adjoining the same; also a Stable, Cart-lodge and Pightle of Land, the whole containing Oa 1r 31p". This was copyhold of the manor of Ludham, fine certain. The apportioned land-tax was 4s, the quit-rent ls 6d and the tithe-rent charge to the vicar was 1s 10d. This was known as the Town Mill and stood in Lovers Lane at the

LUDHAM PARISH

ROYAL GARRETT'S FARM AUCTION 1857

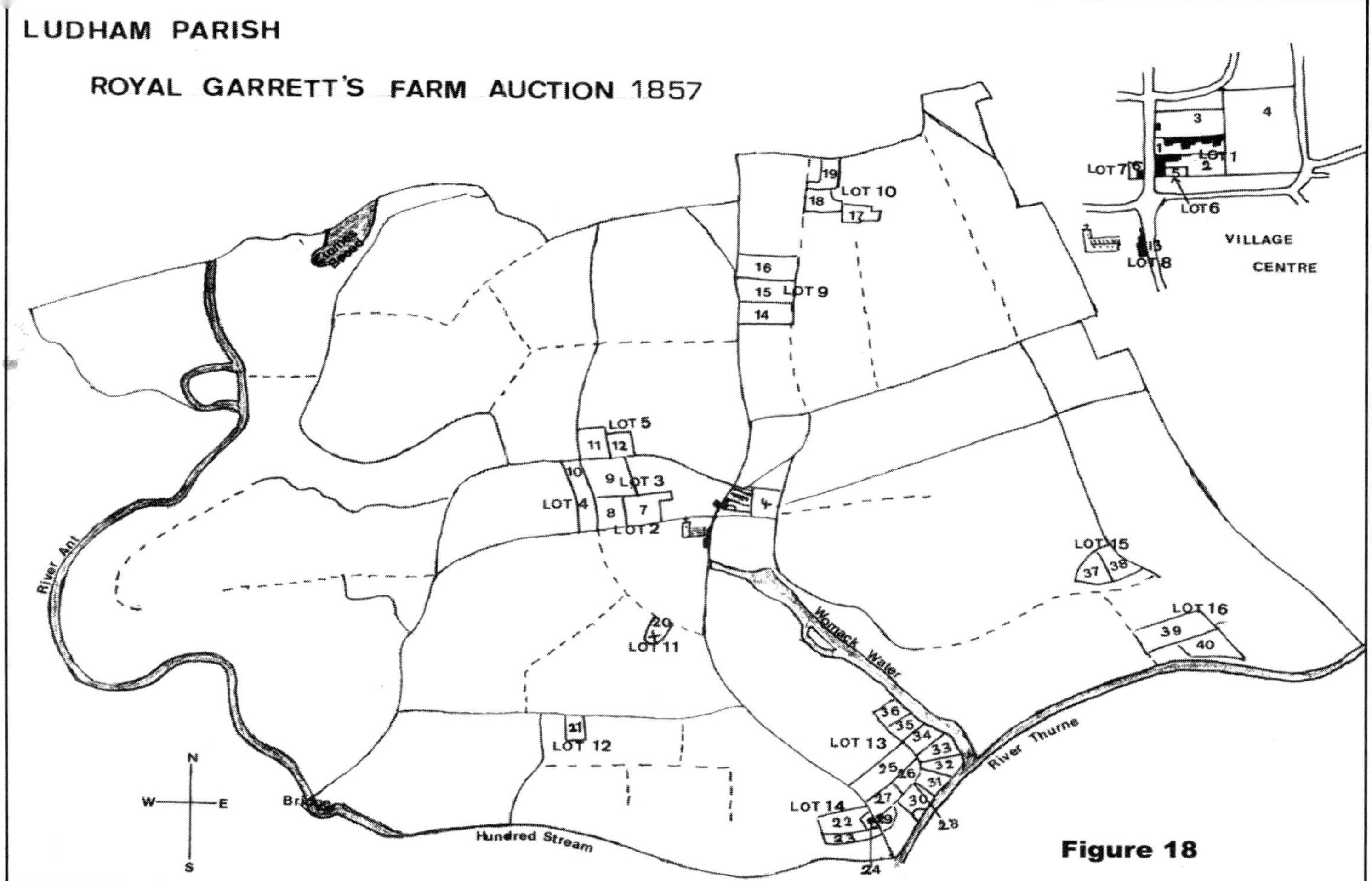

Figure 18

end of the garden of The Homestead, where once Charlie Thompson had his nursery garden and greenhouses. A circular shape where the mill stood might still be visible.

The remaining lots, except the last, were all land. Lot 17 offered the Impropriate Tithe Commutation Rent-charge of £11 1 s 7d, payable from the land numbered 9, 1O, 11 , 12 and 26 on the plan. Which meant that the sum above was to be paid annually to whoever bought Lot 17, and a smaller sum to the vicar, the tithe rents belonging partly to the vicarage of Ludham, under a lease held from the Bishop of Norwich, for terms of twenty-one years and renewable every seven years. The new owner, or impropriator, would be liable to pay the expenses of renewal and the lease, namely 15s 5d every year. Every piece of land in the sale was subject to a tithe-rent charge, payable by its new owner, but the buyer of Lot 17 would only buy the income from the Tithe, but not the land.

All the land offered in this sale was good, fertile farming land, with marsh and meadow at Coldharbour and Fritton. New owners had to pay drainage rates where these applied and also honour any rights of way or other easements.

It would be interesting to know who bought what and also what the four Garrett sons decided to do after the farm was no longer theirs.

Sources:
Sale particulars from Beulah Gowing.
John Garrett. York. Descendant of the Garrett family.

1858, New Vicarage Built

The building that we know today as the Old Vicarage and now used as a residential home for the elderly was built in 1858 when Henry Walker was vicar. It is a nice example of a mid-Victorian house. It cost £820 to build and for this a mortgage was taken out, of which there was a counterpart in the church chest. This was finally paid off thirty years later, in 1888.

The site upon which it was built was a field of about 3 acres known as Broomscroft, which extended from the Norwich Road to School Road. Today the northern part is a housing estate. This field was glebe land and formed part of the 29 acres that the vicar could farm or let out for his own benefit. Being the piece of glebe nearest to the church, it was an obvious place for a vicarage.

It was not the first vicarage upon this site. A very much earlier one had been demolished there in 1666. In the glebe terrier for 1706 it says:

"Piece 1, 3 acres. The Vicarage Dwelling-House being pulled down, George Thomason, clerk, late vicar there, and by him sold and converted to his own use about 40 years ago. There now remains only a small Barn with the Yards and homestalls....."

After this, for about 140 years, the vicars of Ludham lived outside the parish. It is not known where George Thomason, who demolished the ancient vicarage, or his successor, William Baker, lived. Next came Nathanial Hindle, instituted vicar at Ludham on August 7th 1675. It does not say, in the register, where his first two children were born, but the two last ones were born and baptised at Hickling, so perhaps they were living there in the 1680s. His wife, Deborah, died at Potter Heigham vicarage in 1707. All the family are buried in Ludham church at "the vicar's pew door".

Three more vicars came and went, including Richard Tapps, who resigned after only three months. Then came Dudley Butts. who definitely lived at Potter Heigham vicarage. During his time the livings of Potter and Ludham were united. Then also, the small barn left on the site of the demolished vicarage was pulled down.

Plate 48. The Victorian Vicarage, built in 1858. Photograph taken for the author by Broadland Photographics.

Plate 49. The house in Staithe Road used as a vicarage from the early 1800s until 1858. Then it later became the Spread Eagle public house, then a lodging house, then a Temperance Hotel by 1900. The small building with the tall chimney was the communal bake house, now half demolished. Photograph, Clifford Mumby, 1996.

There is a note in the glebe terrier of 1774; "Note, the small barn mentioned in this last terrier (1760) which had been kept up hitherto at much Expence. was become now, by Length of Time in such a ruinous condition, and so greatly decayed in its Timbers, Walls and Roof, that it was judged not capable of being supported and kept in Repair any longer, and being of no Service or Advantage to the Living, but looked upon rather as a Burthen and Incumbrance on the same, upon a Representation thereof to the Rt Revd. Phillip, Lord Bishop of Norwich, as Ordinary and Patron of the Living, it was with his free leave and consent wholly taken down in October 1773".

Next, John Jeffrey became vicar of both Potter and Ludham in 1779 and lived at Potter. Nine years later, after his death, Thomas Leighton was instituted vicar of both parishes. The following year, for reasons that I do not know, the livings of Potter and Ludham were parted and Leighton was re-instituted as vicar of Ludham only. It is interesting to note that, almost 200 years later, the two livings were once again united in 1979.

At the beginning of the nineteenth century the vicar was John Oldershaw, instituted in 1795. He was also vicar of Ranworth with Upton and rector of Redenhall and Harleston. He must have been busy, so he had a curate, Edward Jermyn, who was paid £31 10s a year. Jermyn was followed by Thomas Marshall B.A., who was much better paid at £80 a year and was both curate of Ludham and of Ranworth cum Upton.

In the early years of the nineteenth century a house in Staithe Road began to be used as the vicarage and continued as such for the next fifty years. It was the three storey thatched house (see photograph 49) which has its back to the churchyard and next to the little bakehouse with its tall chimney.

In 1833 Walter Apsley Bathurst became vicar and lived in this house. Both the tithe map schedule of 1842 and the census returns of 1851 confirm this. The latter describes him as a batchelor of 42, born in Middlesex. He had two servants in the house. In 1839 he fathered a son by Clarissa Fairhead, a single woman, seven years his junior, who kept a small general store nearby and who lived with her brothers, George, a carrier and James, a wheelwright. One can imagine the talk that this must have caused in the village... The son, named Walter after his father, died in 1904 and is buried in the churchyard.

In 1855 Henry Walker became vicar and three years later, as we have seen, the new Victorian Vicarage was built. He, and successive vicars, lived there for just over 100 years, until the present new vicarage was built at the gates of the old one.

There was a letter in the church chest, dated August 15 1859, written to Henry Walker from a Mr Bouverie, a lawyer. Having moved into his new vicarage from Staithe Road, Mr Walker must have been concerned that the house there still had a rear door which opened directly into the churchyard. Mr Bouverie's letter states that this door had been there for 35 years when the house was a residence for vicar or curate and that it should have been bricked up when they ceased to be there. The door is still there.

The Staithe Road house continued to have interesting uses; it became the Spread Eagle public house, then a lodging house, then a Temperance hotel.

Sources:
Glebe terriers in church register, 1706 and 1774.
Institution book.
Beulah Gowing.

1867, The High Street Methodist Chapel Built

Plate 50. Old Postcard by W. J. Neave, showing Methodist Chapel and Ludham Street.

At Easter 1967, the Ludham High Street Methodist Church celebrated their centenary. One hundred and one years previously the foundation stone was laid for the building and the 1967 Centenary Celebration Booklet gives a good account of that day, itself taken from the Yarmouth Independent of April 7, 1866, as follows:

"Good Friday was a high day with the inhabitants of Ludham. For two days previously friends had been actively preparing for a demonstration and no little anxiety was manifested about the weather. Early in the morning, flags were hoisted at all the prominent points and by noon streams of visitors poured into the village.

At 2 p.m. a procession, headed by the Sunday School children and teachers, formed outside the old Chapel and, after singing a hymn, marched to the site of the new building, situated in the most eligible spot that could possibly be selected and which, together with the carting of the materials and a donation of £25, is the gift of Aaron Neave Esq. Owing to the admirable arrangements, nearly the whole of the five or six hundred people assembled were enabled to witness the ceremony. Another hymn was followed by a comprehensive prayer by Rev. G. Barnley, Superintendent of the Yarmouth Circuit, who afterwards, in the unavoidable absence of his co-pastor, Rev. W. Hamar, through illness, read 1 Chronicles, chapter 29, verses 1 to 15 and Ephesians, chapter 2. The hymn commencing, "Thou who hast in Zion laid, the true foundation stone", was next sung with admirable effect to the tune "Spanish Chant". A record of the day's proceedings was then read by Mr. J.R. Cossons, the secretary, and afterwards deposited, sealed in a bottle, in a cavity of the stone, with a Circuit Plan, the "Watchman" and "Recorder" (both Wesleyan journals), the "Norfolk News" and the "Yarmouth Independent".

The Rev. G. Barnley, on behalf of the Trustees, presented a beautifully engraved silver trowel to Wm. Twitchell Esq., of Willington, near Bedford. Mr Twitchell then proceeded to lay the foundation stone in the name of the Holy Trinity.

The Rev. G. Barnley spoke at length upon the doctrines and polity of Wesleyan Methodism. The corner stones were then laid by the following young ladies:- Miss Neave, Miss L. Skinner, Miss Hacon and Miss Huke. Memorial stones were also placed by Mrs Twitchell, Mrs Tuttle and others. Then the school children advanced in single file and deposited on the stones purses containing the sums they had collected and, after singing right heartily and with true Methodist loyalty a verse of the National Anthem, a large portion of the assembly repaired to Mr Neave's farm and did ample justice to a beautiful tea provided by the kindness of the ladies."

In the evening there was a meeting in a barn. Mr Twitchell presided and there were many speakers and a numerous company. Stirring addresses were delivered by several and a vote of thanks to Messrs. Neave, Twitchell and Tuttle (who had laboured indefatigably in the preparations) brought a happy day to its end.

The cost of building had been estimated at £350 and the builder and architect was Mr Chaplin of Ludham. This estimate was too small and the final cost was £565, and when the Chapel was opened in the summer of 1867 the entire sum had been raised.

The Centenary Booklet adds that the bottle was recently recovered from the foundation stone, but sadly, the contents were mouldy and of no value.

Source :
Centenary Celebration Booklet of Ludham High Street Methodist Church, Easter 1967, kindly supplied to me by Bill and Kathleen Sloper.

Plate 51. Aaron Neave's Town Farm where the chapel tea took place. This later became Harriot England's grocery shop. Note the chapel in the background. Photograph, the author.

Plate 52. Staithe Road. The roofs and chimneys of the now vanished Town House Row cottages just visible over the hedge. Why is a flag flying on the distant house? It would have been a Temperence Hotel about the time of this old postcard.

1870, The Town House

A terrier of the Town Lands was made in 1706 and written into the church register of 1685-1739. It ends with a reference to: "The Town House, adjoining upon the Churchyard walls in six several apartments, inhabited by the Poor of the said Town".

This was the parish poor house where lived the aged or homeless poor, six little dwellings, right against the south-east corner of the churchyard, and fronting on to Staithe Road. It was condemned and demolished by the District Council in about 1954, and I am ashamed to say that not only did I not photograph it, but I cannot even remember what it looked like.

However, Violet Bensley has given me a description; the cottages were cement-rendered brick with tiled roofs. Each had one room up and one down, with a large pantry cum kitchen. The stairs were narrow and the floors uneven and there was a large beam across the ceiling. The water supply was a pump in the yard and there was an earth closet in the shed. In the 1950's there were only four dwellings, but in earlier times, after the buildings were in private hands, it is possible that the two northern ones were demolished, to be replaced by the present house which stands there, and of which the garden was the site of the other four.

In 1790 the Town House was sold for £50 clear of all expenses. The money was invested in the Smallburgh Union House of Industry, from which sum the Directors and Guardians paid 5% interest on Christmas day each year to the Ludham churchwardens and overseers to be used for the relief of the poor.

Nearly a hundred years later, in 1870, there was a letter from Smallburgh Union to the churchwardens and overseers, returning to them the original sum of £50. This was because the local Act by which the Incorporation of Tunstead and Happing had been governed, had been repealed and it became necessary to return the money in order to release the Union from all debts and incumbrances.

The Union suggested in the letter that the proper course would be to invest the money in Public Funds, say 3% Consols, and then the dividend could be used for poor relief as the interest had previously been used. This was done and there is a certificate for Consolidated Annuities dated December 2, 1870. During the 1950's and 60's when I was secretary to the Poors' Land Trust, the money was still in 3% Consols and it brought in the princely sum of £1.6.8. per annum, less than when it was invested in the work-house.....!

From 1790 then, the dwellings were in private ownership and were rented out. In the rate book of 1878 the owner is Thomas Fitt and the cottages were known as the Town Row.

Sources:
Mrs Violet Bensley, Ludham.
The church register of 1685 to 1739.
A rate book of 1878.
Letter from Smallburgh Union of 1870.
Share certificate of 1870.

1871, Demolition of the Pound

Until 23 March 1871, the Ludham pound stood at the cross-roads on the Norwich Road, upon the site now occupied by "Crossways", beside Love Lane with Pound Lane opposite.

A pound was an enclosure where straying cattle were impounded, and a fine had to be paid to recover one's cattle. The pinder was the village official in charge of the pound. It was a symbol of the old medieval open field system; where there were no hedges or fences and cattle often strayed. After enclosure the need for a pound diminished. The Ludham one was built of brick with gates and a wooden coping on top of the walls.

There is a letter from the vicar, the Rev. Walker, and a reply from the Ecclesiastical Commissioners stating that the removal was approved by the Surveyor of Highways, that it was thought advantageous to remove it and that there was no proposal to restore it. The land upon which it stood belonged to the Church Commissioners at that time, being then part of the Hall Farm lands and it was called Church Close.

The demolition took two days and it was done by Mr Heath's men from the Hall Farm, at the direction of Sir William Forster, steward of the manor.

It is not known when that particular pound had been built, but there was a pound in Ludham as early as 1305, though perhaps not in the same place. In the church register of 1685-1739 is copied an agreement between the Abbot of St Benets and Lord Abergavenny in 1305. Both being lords of manors in Ludham, Catfield and Potter Heigham, they had often disagreed upon the amount of profit that each should take from the manors. They finally agreed that the Abbot should have two parts profit and Lord Abergavenny one part. They also decided that a pound should be built "in a convenient place upon some part of the Wast there at Ludham and that the Cattel found in and upon the said Wast shall be impounded in the said Pound and not elsewhere". Lord Abergavenny was to find a full third of the cost of erecting and maintaining the pound and the Abbot two thirds, the future profit thereof, from the fines, to be divided in the same way.

It is hardly likely that the field belonging to the Abbey farm would have been described as waste land, so that earlier pound must have been elsewhere. It was surely made of wood, so it is unlikely to have left any trace today, but it must have been in a fairly central position in the parish for convenience.

Sources:
Letter from the Rev. Henry Walker.
Church register 1685-1739.

1873, The Board School Built

In 1870 an Act of Parliament for Elementary Education was passed in England and Wales, which provided for the formation of Board Schools in different districts and for the compulsory attendance of children there.

In Ludham a school board of five members was formed in 1872, the clerk being Horatio Girdlestone, a tailor by trade. A year later the Board School was built with room for 140 children, at a cost of £1,350. It opened on January 5th 1874 with Mrs Annie Harwood as the headmistress.

The school is built of brick, in Victorian gothic style with a slate roof and metal decorations, since removed, along the ridges. Over windows and doorways are patterns of coloured bricks and the west porch has a panel with the date 1873. Under all the eaves is a band of decorated brickwork. The boys and girls had separate playgrounds with a wall between them. The infants went in the girls' playground. There was also a separating wall in the front yard. In 1875 a house was built in the same style right next to the school, for the head teacher.

In 1891 there was an offer from the government to help Elementary Schools to abolish fees, but no school board was obliged to accept this. The Ludham board decided in favour of the move and after the summer holidays of 1891, the school opened free of all charge. I do not know what the fees were previously, but children at the National School, founded in 1841, paid a penny a week for labourers' children, twopence for journeymens' and threepence for tradesmens' children. This older school continued to exist alongside the new Board School for some years, as it is mentioned in a rate book of 1879.

But it must have closed between then and 1892 as the new school had to be enlarged in that year, by the addition of a classroom. This cost £600 and enabled 200 children to attend the school, of which the average attendance was 120.

In the 1890's David Edwards was the headmaster. Arthur Newton, born in 1886 and a pupil there, remembered him; "He

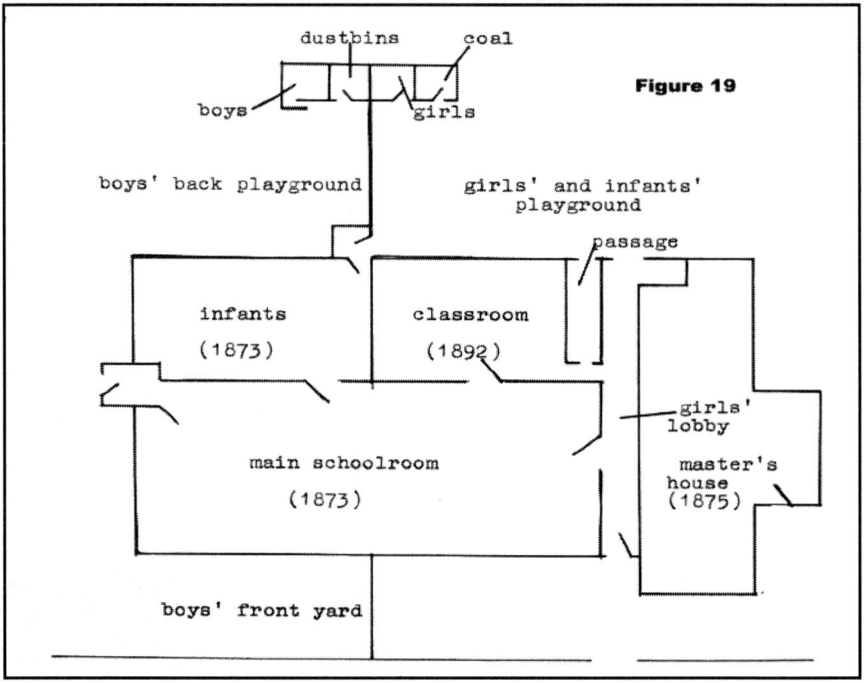

Sketch Plan of Ludham School, c. 1911, not to scale.

was a brute! His wife was just as bad. They were got rid of and Mr. Hayhurst followed, that was jolly nice!" George Hayhurst was headmaster from 1896 until 1924 and was much loved. His wife joined him as a teacher during this time. Mrs A.B. Dale was infant teacher. Mrs Kittle was still teaching there until she retired on November 10, 1899 after 27 years and was replaced by Miss L. M. Feathers.

The second school log-book, which was kindly lent to me by Arthur Bird, headmaster from 1944 to 1971, begins in October 1899, right at the end of the nineteenth century. But no doubt school events in the early twentieth century were little different from those of the final years of the previous one. Absence for farm work was a continual theme in a village school and the arrangement of school terms was originally made to allow the corn harvest to be brought in before the long holidays ended in September.
Our present scholastic year is still based upon agriculture!

The school was frequently closed for various reasons; for an Oddfellows Quarterly meeting there in October 1899, the next year a holiday on 25 May was for the Queen's birthday and the Relief of Mafeking, to be rapidly followed by another day off to celebrate the capture of Pretoria on 1 June. Then came the usual holidays in Trinity week for Ludham Fair, and the annual school treat on 14 September. The following year the school was closed while the census was taken on 1 April, for the annual church choir picnic on 22 July and for the chapel outing on 1 August. Mr. Hayhurst notes in the log-book that it would be better if all denominations had their outings on the same day, and that a Friday, which is what did happen later on.

Plate 53.
Is this Ludham school? Is this Miss Feathers with her class?
The photograph was given to me by Ethel Grounds, born 1901, who went to Ludham school, so it should be, but her daughters do not recognise their mother in the picture. Beulah Gowing and the author both think that she is the pretty little girl at top left. The brickwork of Ludham school is of single stretchers; the brickwork shown above, of double stretchers for one header, is the same as a wall beside the school of a vanished barn.

During the winters the school rooms became very cold. At 10 a.m. one December day, the thermometer registered 42 F. It was resolved to close the school early during the winter months, any time after 3.30 p.m., as some children had a long journey home on foot in the dark. In December two boys had to go to East Ruston for exams. They left at 6 a.m. and walked a total of 12 miles there and back.

At a board meeting on 19 July, 1900, the chairman and vice-chairman both addressed the school children and urged a need for greater effort and regularity of attendance. The chairman added, "I would that some of the ladies of the village would take a lively interest in the school work of some of the girls. Visits during the exams would be appreciated by the whole school".

On 3 August, 1900 it was announced that the school holidays would begin on 6 August instead of on 9 August as planned, "because of the more rapid ripening of the corn than anticipated". Children were often absent because they were helping with some job on a farm. Sometimes in July the whole school closed for two weeks for fruit picking. The childrens' wages were vital for the poorer families, and from the farmer's point of view, the quicker the crop was gathered in, the better.

Mr Hayhurst once caught some children helping themselves to turnips from the field next to the school. (Imagine a modern child enjoying a piece of turnip...) He put one boy into the coal shed as a punishment, then forgot all about him. Mrs Hayhurst set him free at 4.30 p.m. "From this time, if I have cause, I will confine children in the house", wrote Mr Hayhurst afterwards.

A problem of verminous hair made him suggest that girls should wear their hair tied back. One or two still came to school with their hair loose, so he sent them home to have it tied, but they did not return. The next day one brought a letter. "Sir, it is quite useless for you to send Annie home to have her hair tied back for I will not tie it back for any Liberal, Tory or any government. If her head was dirty and alive with vermin you would have good reason to send her home. If she is sent home she will not return to school again until you either come or send for her." In order to maintain discipline he felt bound to tell the children to return home.

He was proved right later, when at the first authorised medical inspection in 1909, all hair was completely free from vermin, which was attributed to the enforced rule of tying back hair.

The school did not then own the large field at the back, now used as the recreation ground, so Mrs Fitzhugh at The Grange kindly offered the use of her meadow for games, and also presented the school with a football. This was much appreciated and the meadow was used a lot, the annual sports also being held there. (See Plate 55) Today Ludham School is still going strong after 125 years, though many things are different now. At the Centenary celebrations held in 1973, I signed the visitors' book and was proud to put in the column headed "In what capacity have you known the school?" - parent, canteen worker and school manager.

Sources:
The second school log-book, 1899 to the present day.
Kindly lent by Arthur Bird, headmaster.

Plate 54. The West Porch. Photograph, Clifford Mumby.

Plate 55. Ludham Sports Day on Mrs Fitzhugh's field c.1900.
Photographs given to me by Mrs Albert England.

Trade and Industry in Ludham.

After agriculture, the most important industry in Ludham was brickmaking. There was a good source of brick-earth clay on top of the Yarmouth Road hill, just east of the mill. This was known as The Earthhole and it was dug out to a depth of several feet over quite a large area. The earliest brick kiln is in the field just to the south-east of the hole. It is underground and was only discovered when Mr Goodwin's tractor went through into a space below and exposed small brick arches, vitrified with heat. A Castle Museum representative said it was probably seventeenth or eighteenth century.

The next, and largest, kiln was on Womack Staithe. There were two large arches there until the 1960s, but the conical chimney had crumbled some time before. James Green at Beeches Farm was the owner of this at the end of the nineteenth century and also of the large malthouse next to it. Margaret Keeler, born 1908, said that her grandfather, Charles Wilkerson, came from Wroxham in 1877 to work for Green as a maltster and brickmaker. When the malting season was over, he became foreman of the brickyard at Womack.

An average workman could make 1500 bricks a day. First he roughly worked the clay with a spade and water. Then he filled the brick-shaped moulds exactly and levelled off the top. After he had dusted them with dry clay the bricks stood for nine days if the weather was dry and then they were fired. The Womack kiln could burn 32,000 bricks at a time. The bricks were stacked on the staithe to await transport by wherries. Moulded bricks had no standard size. They could be ornamented with patterns or cut and rubbed to shapes. Small holes in them were caused by exploding chalk. Non-moulded bricks were made of clay laid on straw, flattened and cut into blocks. These fired unevenly. It is interesting to see that the lower part of the back of the malthouse is built of badly fired bricks. Presumably these were no use for selling and so came in handy. The third, and much smaller brick kiln was on top of How Hill, just past the mill house, where there is a slight depression at the roadside.

Another local industry was malting barley. The best barley is grown in Norolk and makes good beer.

Plate 56.

The Earthhole.

Source of clay for bricks. Access down from left.

High Mill (Ludham Mill) in background, converted 1932.

Photographs, the author.

Plate 57.

The First Brick Kiln is under this field from where the photograph was taken.

The thatched house was called Hill Farm.

Plate 58.

Womack Malt-house.

Photograph taken as it was being converted into flats.

Photographs, the author.

Plate 59.

Womack Brick Kiln.

Taken in the 1960s just before demolition; the conical chimney had already gone.

Plate 60. Staithe House and the old Staithe. Storage sheds for merchandise. The wherry is the Early Bird.

The original malthouse was just north of the village. William Hacon of Malthouse Farm was a farmer and maltster who employed 10 men. He built the Grange in 1839 on the site of Malthouse Farm. On the 1842 tithe map there are numerous buildings to the north of this, on what was then called Malthouse Lane, turning off the Catfield Road.

The large malthouse at Womack is not marked on that map, but James Green, maltster and brickworks was at Beeches Farm at that time. The malthouse is a fine building, which has been saved by being turned into holiday flats.

Another industry, boatbuilding, took place further along Horse Fen Road, where the Harrisons, father and son, had their yard. Robert Harrison, senior, lived in Fenside, and his son, Robert, in a house nearer the water. The late Mr Horace Bolingbroke kindly gave me the photograph, taken in 1881, showing a wherry undergoing repairs under a rather frail-looking roof. They built the wherry Zoe here in 1873.

Plate 61. *Harrisons' Boat Yard, Womack, 1881.*
Photograph by the late Horace Bolingbroke.

River-borne trade was very important during the nineteenth century, and Ludham was well placed for this with its boundary of rivers at the centre of the river system. The staithes there were always busy, at How Hill, Ludham Bridge and Womack. Almost everything was conveyed by wherry; bricks, reed, manure, marl, sand, lime, as well as the more domestic goods like coal, beer, paraffin oil and other items. At Staithe House, John Clarke was a merchant who dealt in the latter things, and there was a customs and excise officer at his house, as smuggling was not unknown... At that time the wherries could come right up to the road, and the goods were loaded into horse-drawn carts to be delivered in the parish.

In the village, Englands, the millwrights, had their workshops from which they built mills all over Norfolk. There was a wheelwright's and carpenter's workshop behind the Norwich Road cottages, where carts and wheels and other wooden things were made. Three or four blacksmiths were always busy and George Knights made horse collars and harness in his little shop opposite the church, having taken over from James Lacey in 1871.

Plate 62. Ludham Street, showing Clarissa Fairhead's shop on far right, at the time of the photograph belonging to C. Clarke. Next door is Grace Lyon's bigger shop. On the left a large board marks the entrance to the Kings Arms Bowling green. Old postcard.

Of the shops, Clarissa Fairhead still kept her little general store which she had owned since at least 1839 and she was to continue until the end of the century.

On the site of the present day butcher's shop next door, Mr and Mrs Fred Lyon had taken over from John Bayles in 1876. Plate 63 shows the original shop window, which had been modernised when the preceding photograph was taken.

Plate 63. Grace Lyon's Shop. Photograph given to me by Grace Lyon's daughter, the late Constance Wright.

At the far end of the Street Harriot England, widow of William Kirby England, ran a grocery shop in the white thatched house that used to be called Town Farm; she had bought it with the compensation money for the loss of her husband, who had died of his injuries after a mill accident in 1857. This later became Cook's shop.

Another grocer and draper was William Vince. One presumes that he followed William Fendick during the late nineteenth century at what is now Thrower's supermarket.

Plate 64. Ludham Street. On the right is Thrower's shop, previously Vince's and Fendick's. Next door in a low building, is Kirby England's butcher's shop with a sign showing a fat bullock. Old postcard.

When Albert and Helen Thrower took on this shop in 1902, they were taking over a twice bankrupt business.

It is amusing to note from the pictures that one shop sold Lyon's tea, another Mazawattee tea and a third Lipton's. One wonders what tea Mrs England sold...

Mrs England's son Kirby had the butcher's shop in the village centre, which continued until recent years. Mary Ann Clarke's butcher's shop at Albury House continued until 1900. Somewhere in Ludham a Mr French supplied 61 lbs of salt beef at the Queen's jubilee in 1887. In 1883 the aptly named Mrs Mary Pigg seems to have replaced her late husband as pork butcher, in one of the Yarmouth Road thatched houses.

Fish was sold from the smokehouse in a wooden shed opposite the Church Room which belonged to John and Eldred Slaughter.

At the Kings Arms, the brewers, Youngs and Co., were the owners and Daniel England had taken over as landlord in 1883. Mrs Julia Willgress was landlady at the Rose and Crown during the 1880s and then Eldred Slaughter became the last licensee there before it ceased to be a public house in 1900.

Across the road at the Bakers Arms beer house, Walter Lincoln was the occupier and it was owned by Buntings Executive. Down Staithe Road, the Spread Eagle, once the vicarage, was still a pub, but not for much longer, for it became a Temperance lodging house around the turn of the century. John Clarke of Staithe House owned it in 1879. The Dog Inn, down towards the bridge, was owned by the brewers, Steward and Patterson,and was kept by a landlady, Mrs Charlotte Bunn.

By 1889 the Post Office had moved to a cottage in the Norwich Road row. John Thurgate combined being a blacksmith and a sub-postmaster. Mail arrived from Norwich at 8 a.m. and was delivered in the parish at 2.35 p.m. on weekdays and 10.25 a.m. on Sundays. Thomas Thurgate drove the carrier's cart to the Waggon and Horses in Norwich on Mondays, Wednesdays and Saturdays.

Did the coming of the railway nearby during the 1880s make a difference to Ludham trade and industry? The station at Potter Heigham was about two miles away. It was probably more convenient to continue to have goods sent and delivered by wherry to the staithes right near the village than to go to the station.

Practically everything that one could need was available in Ludham at that time. Far more than today, in fact. Given the economic climate in the 1880s and 1890s, it seems surprising that so many businesses - four grocers, four butchers and five pubs could all survive, but obviously some did not last much longer.

Sources:
Robert Malster, "Wherries and Waterways", 1971, Terence Dalton Ltd.
Kelly's directories, 1883 and 1888.
Chesney England.
Beulah Gowing.
Ludham Rate Book, 1879.

Plate 65. The Yarmouth Road into Ludham with the Kings Arms in the centre and the demolished Bakers Arms on the right. Old Postcard.

1883 - 1894, From Vestry Meeting to Parish Council.

The vestry meeting was the ancient assembly of all the parishioners, originally held in the church vestry and which levied the church rate. This meeting gradually took the place of the manor and hundred courts and eventually levied other rates and elected and controlled the parish officers. An act of parliament in 1818 for "The Regulation of Parish Vestries" made more changes, among which, only those who paid rates might attend and there must be a minute book and a chairman to sign it. The following are a few extracts from the minute book for the last of the Ludham vestry meetings before the parish council came into being, created by the Local Government Act of 1893.

In 1883 the vestry minute book gives the amounts of poor rate levied during that year.

January 4	Poor rate 5d in the pound.
April 19	Poor rate 6d in the pound.
June 28	Poor rate 7d in the pound.
October18	Poor rate 5d in the pound.

In 1885 there is a list of the parish officers elected for that year. They were : -

Vicar's churchwarden -	Thomas Slipper.
Peoples' churchwarden -	Robert Clarke.
Overseers of the Poor -	John Kittle.
	James Grapes.
Parish Constables -	George S. Knights.
	Charles Blaxell.
Surveyor of Highways -	Herbert Hacon.

At the end of the century the Norfolk County Council was taking over maintenance and responsibility for various roads in the county. The Ludham meeting obviously thought it a good idea if they and their surveyor of highways could be relieved of the burden of what we now know as the main road through Ludham, for at the meeting in August 1889 it was proposed and seconded that the road from Ludham bridge to the Potter Heigham boundary, known as the Norwich and Yarmouth Road, be handed over to the County Council. The parish surveyor of highways, Mr Ben Kittle, was instructed to apply to the council for this.

The N.C.C. must have thought that the road was not in a good enough condition for them to accept, for at a meeting of the vestry in 1890 it "was agreed to allow the surveyor of highways to spend £50 on repair of the Norwich and Yarmouth Road, in order to make the same road in condition good enough for the N.C.C. to take over". At the same time, the N.C.C. invited the parish to make over to them about 2 furlongs of the Yarmouth-Stalham road. This was the tiny portion of Long Lane which crosses Ludham parish in the north-eastern corner, between the parishes of Potter Heigham and Catfield. Mr Ben Kittle was instructed to apply for this and the chairman, the Rev. J.J. Willmott, was asked to find out the exact conditions under which the N.C.C. took over roads to make them into main roads.

Two years later, in March 1892, they were still discussing roads and the surveyor of highways was told to apply for the N.C.C. to take over the road from Catfield boundary to the turn of the Norwich Road by the gate known as Mr J. Kittle's White Gate. This was Goffin's Lane, then round by the older council houses to what is still called White Gate Corner. It seems curious that they wanted this road taken over, rather than the main Catfield Road.

In 1893 at the March vestry meeting, Dr Gordon said that he would see the postmaster at Norwich with regard to irregular delivery of letters in the parish and the time of delivery, and also to consider the question of Sunday delivery and its abolition in Ludham.

1894 saw the last vestry meeting and it is recorded in the minute book that the parochial electors met in the Board School room to receive nomination papers of those entitled to serve on the first parish council. Thirteen were received, for nine places.
They were. Bond, Howell, Lake, Leather, Lemon, Morgan, Newton, Page, Sikes, Watson, Wilkerson, Willmott and Vince.

Unfortunately there were no details of that first election. In the beginning, the parish council was re-elected every year. It is still going strong just over a hundred years later, but there are now eleven members, as the population has increased.

Sources:
Ludham vestry meeting minute book. N.R.O.

1884, The Piano Tuner's Bill

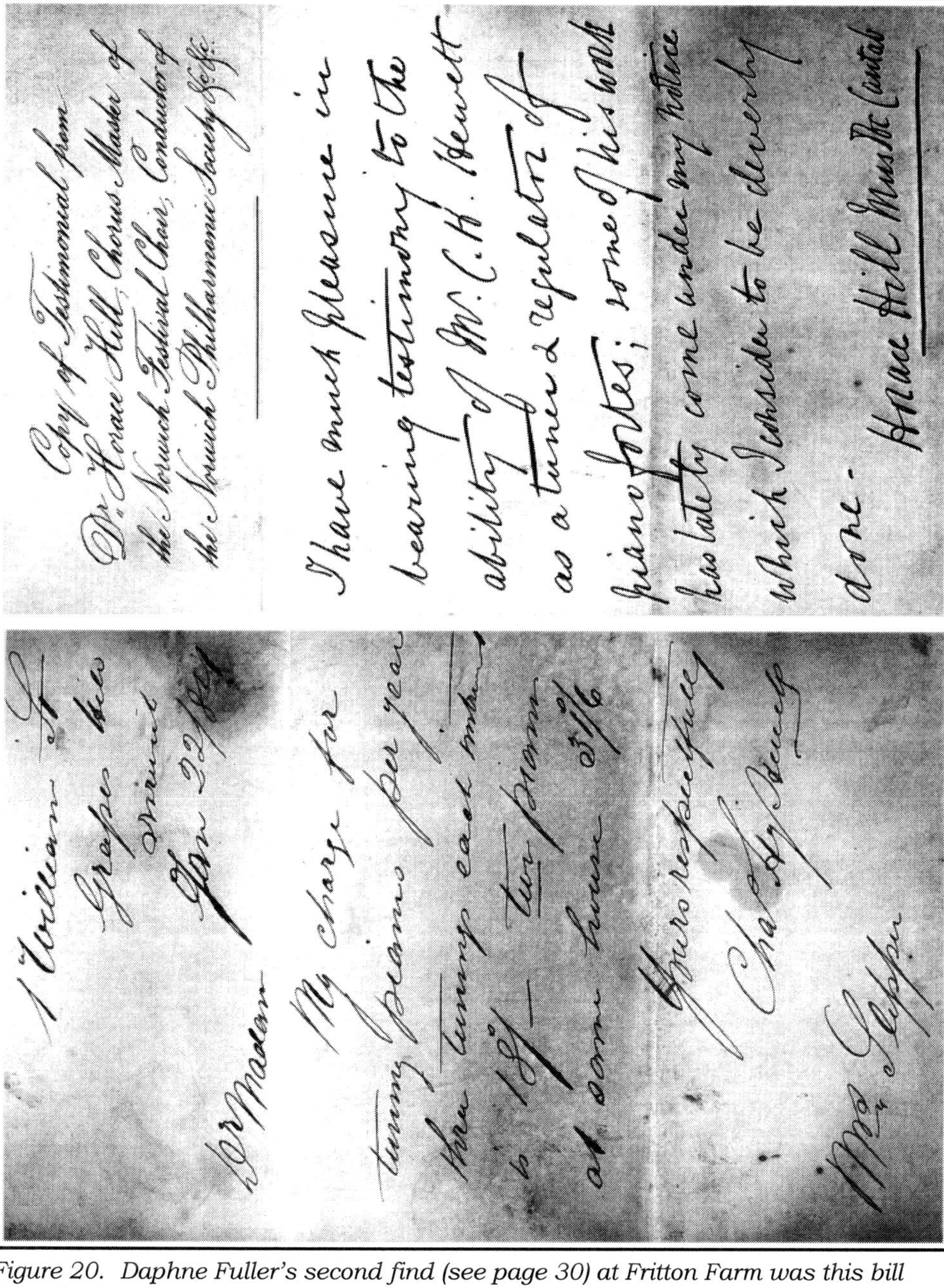

Copy of Testimonial from
Dr. Horace Hill, Chorus Master of
the Norwich Festival Choir, Conductor of
the Norwich Philharmonic Society &c. &c.

I have much pleasure in
bearing testimony to the
ability of Mr. C. H. Sewell
as a tuner & regulator of
pianofortes; some of his work
has lately come under my notice
which I consider to be cleverly
done – Horace Hill Mus Bac Cantab

[illegible]
Jan 22 [illegible]

Dr Madam
My charge for
tuning pianos per year
three tunings each [illegible]
is 18/– two pianos
at same house 31/6
Yours respectfully
Chas H Sewell

Mrs Slipper

Figure 20. Daphne Fuller's second find (see page 30) at Fritton Farm was this bill from Chas. H. Sewell piano tuner, to Mrs Slipper in 1884, for tuning two pianos three times. The original is on both sides of a folded paper.

1887, Celebrations for Queen Victoria's Golden Jubilee

Ludham celebrated the Golden Jubilee of Queen Victoria on June 21st 1887 in great style. A committee of eighteen people under the vicar, the Rev. J.J.Willmott, met beforehand and arranged the programme for the day as follows;

1.30 Service in the church.
2.30 Procession, headed by brass band.
5.00 The meal.
10.00 Close.

Six of the committee members canvassed the parish, collected subscriptions and issued 639 tickets. A total of 218 people contributed to the cost, with gifts ranging from sixpence to five pounds. A ladies committee was formed and Dr. Gordon agreed to organise the sports. Mrs Hacon from The Grange gave a white satin rosette to each committee member and a red, white and blue one to the stewards. Mr Baldwin of Laurels Farm offered the use of his barn and a meadow for the celebrations.

The day itself was a great success. Early in the morning a merry peal of bells rang forth from the church tower, from which flew the red, white and blue flag. At 1.30 a large congregation assembled in the church, which was bright with flowers. It was a service of thanksgiving and the text of the sermon was Romans, chapter 13, verse 5.

After the service, all the people, headed by the Gt Yarmouth Temperance Band, went in procession from the church to Laurels Farm. Here, the sports and general fun and games took place on the meadow. For prizes, 100 yards of calico had been bought.

In the barn, which was decorated with flags, flowers and pictures of the Queen, a bountiful provision of good things was spread. 28 stones of beef, weighed in joints of 1 stone each, had been purchased from Mr England and 61 lbs of salt beef from Mr French. There is a list of names of 59 carvers and waiters! In the evening there was more enjoyment with dancing and the band playing, and the day closed with a splendid display of fireworks on the meadow.

The receipts for the goods purchased for this day are interesting; as much as possible was bought in Ludham. Mr Cook supplied 300 large loaves and some small ones. Mrs Lyon sold 30 lbs of loaf sugar, 14 lbs of biscuits and 72 yards of calico, as well as tea and 1¾ lbs of tobacco at 4/- a pound. (Her grocery shop was where the butchers shop is today)

Mr Vince's shop supplied similar goods plus 26 lbs of jam. Still more sugar and tobacco were bought from Mrs Grapes and Mr England supplied all the condiments and more tobacco. 120 lbs of cake were bought in Norwich and more tea from Laddams on The Walk. From Yarmouth came four briar pipes, a carving knife and fork and two silver clocks, which cost 5/6 each.

The best receipt of all is the one for the fireworks from C.T. Brock & Co. It is very decorative and describes the firm as the "Sole Pyrotechnists to the Crystal Palace Co. and the Sultan of Turkey etc". Last, but not least, the Temperance band charged £5.10.0 for their services.

It is rather sad that, ten years later, on the Queen' s Diamond Jubilee in 1897, there were no celebrations in Ludham. A meeting was held and it was reported that many had "expressed their determination not to do anything". So it was decided to let the matter drop.

Why was this? Times were very difficult and most people were too poor for such frivolities. Labourers' wages were very low and many were suffering from want of work, age or poverty. In 1888 five people emigrated from Ludham to the U.S.A. and Canada. The Parish Magazine comments that "emmigration is a good thing for a young man because of lack of work here and overpopulation".

Sources:
Ludham Parish Magazines.
Receipts. N.R.O.

1887, The Death of Samuel Taylor Huke

On 1 July 1887, the following obituary appeared in the Eastern Daily Press, of Samuel Taylor Huke, who had died at Yarmouth on June 27, at the age of 85. Mr Huke had lived at the Manor at Ludham and was the local doctor and medical officer.

" Samuel Tay1or Huke M.R.C.S. Eng., and LSA, son of the late Mr William Huke, builder and millwright, of Great Yarmouth, was born March 23rd, 1802. He served a seven years' apprenticeship to Dr Bateman, a well-known surgeon, and after passing through the usual curriculum at Guys' and St Thomas' Hospitals, London, and taking his degrees in medicine and surgery, he commenced practice in Ludham, Norfolk. where he remained for over 50 years medical officer for the district. When at the hospitals, he had the honour of taking a prize from the hands of the celebrated surgeon, Sir Astley Cooper (also a Yarmouth man), in the form of one of his works just then published (1823) called "A Treatise on Dislocation and Fractures of the Joints". This book Mr Huke most highly valued, not only for its own merit, but because it contains on the fly-leaf the following inscription in Sir Astley's own hand: "A present from Sir Astley Cooper to Samuel Huke on account of his great acquirements in anatomy and surgery".

Deputy-Inspector General McCormick, the well known Arctic and Antarctic traveller, who is still living, and has of late years been a highly esteemed correspondent of Mr Huke's was a fellow pupil with him of Dr Bateman's. He was born in 1800 and so is 2 years his senior.

On retiring from practice in 1875, and coming to Yarmouth, where he has since resided, Mr Huke had several valuable testimonials presented to him, amongst which the one he himself most highly prized was a quarto edition of Mathew Henry's commentaries, together with a silver snuff box, subscribed for voluntarily by the poor people of the district as a token of their affection and esteem, as he was looked upon as one of their greatest friends and benefactors. No weather ever hindered, no trouble prevented him from faithfully attending to them in their necessities, and very often without a prospect of remuneration, as the district in his early days was very poor, labourers' wages being 10s for a married man and 9s for a single one per week. During his long and useful life he was a bright and shining light among the Wesleyans, which body he joined in London, when a student, continuing an active and beloved member to within twelve months of his death. At the same time he was equally admired and esteemed by members of other denominations, as he was no bigot, and often during sickness administered to the welfare of the souls as well as the bodies of the patients. irrespective of class or creed when the services of a minister could not easily be obtained.

In 1831 he married the eldest daughter of the late Mr James Norton of Stokesby, who still survives, at the age of 81 to mourn her loss. Out of a family of fifteen children, but three remain, the eldest being a chemist at Chester and the two others booksellers in the Market Row, Yarmouth."

I am grateful to Eileen Wallace and Jo Wright for finding this obituary in the Eastern Counties Newspapers Library.

-ooOoo-

Firemarks

Figure 21

These plaques, of which there is a good example from the Norwich Union, on a gable of Saddler's cottage, were issued in the early days of insurance. Usually made of lead, sometimes gilded, they cost the policy-holder two shillings and sixpence and were part of the contract, which was not deemed completed until the mark was fixed onto the property insured.

Each had a policy number as well as the emblem of the company. Only that paticular company's fire brigade could put out the fire, and as the fire engine was horsedrawn and in this case would have to come all the way from Norwich, was a pretty hopeless prospect! There is an interesting collection of firemarks in the Bridewell Museum, Norwich

1889 - 1890. Restoration of the Church

The church of St Catherine at Ludham is extremely large for a village church. The size of a church does not necessarily indicate a large population, but rather the wealth of a community. It is also an act of worship, built or enlarged by someone to the glory of God. Throughout the centuries the church at Ludham had close connections with the nearby Abbey of St Benet at Holme.

There must have been an earlier church than the present one on the site, for a charter of c. 1047 from King Edward to St Benets mentions the "church and vill of Ludham with its appurtenances". Ludham church was then a rectory, valued at 43 marks, (about £32.25) until on June 6, 1220 the church revenues were appropriated to the Abbey, with the consent of Bishop Pandulf and confirmed by the Pope. This meant that the abbot became rector of the parish and took the great tithes, and the vicar of the parish, appointed by the abbot, had only the small tithes. (see Commutation of Tithes, page 45) It is because of this event in 1220 that the Ecclesiastical Commissioners are today still responsible for the repair of the chancel at Ludham and the present Bishop of Norwich, who is also abbot of St Benets is the rector and patron of the benefice.

The present building has a tower and chancel built during the fourteenth century in decorated style, showing that it was already a large church by that time. The east window is a lovely example of reticulated, or fish-net, tracery. There is a priest's door to the chancel with a scratch dial on the buttress beside it, which indicated the time of the next mass with a pointer.

At some time during the fifteenth century the nave and aisles were rebuilt in the perpendicular style, with one window, next to the south porch, later than the rest, with more pronounced perpendicular tracery and four lights. That the earlier nave and aisles had been as large as the building that replaced them, is shown by the finding of earlier buttress foundations during the making of the drainage trench round the north side in 1890. Also the inside arches to both porch doors are thirteenth century.

Plate 66. (above)

Priest's Door to Chancel. The Scratch Dial is marked on the Buttress.
Photograph, the author.

Plate 67. (right)

The Scratch Dial.
Photograph, old church guide.

Plate 68.

Ancient chest, with lid made from a Hollowed Tree.

Photograph, old church guide.

Plate 69.

The East Window.

Photograph, the author.

Plate 70. Old postcard of the Church seen from the Old Staithe.

During the nineteenth century the church was well used with large congregations and long sermons. At a confirmation service in 1888 for 74 candidates, the bishop even gave two addresses.

By the middle of that century the church building was becoming shabby and in need of repair. The British Archaeological Association visited Ludham church in July 1879, led by Mr Loftus-Brock, when they lunched at the Crown Inn. In the account of their visit, the architectural features of the church are much admired, but they also noticed "rickety deal pews" and a "broken and decayed ancient poor box, full of filthy cobwebs". They also made an extraordinary discovery; hidden in the rood-loft stairs they found some plain oak panels covered in whitewash. The shapes of the panels suggested that they might fit the chancel arch. When some whitewash was cleaned off, paintings of the crucifixion of Christ and other figures were found! These boards were removed to the vicarage by the Rev. Henry Walker for safe keeping, and where they were to remain for the next 13 years.

*Plate 71. The Tympanum Boards on the Chancel Floor in 1969 During Restoration by Mr. J.L. Royal F.I.I.C.
Photograph, the author.*

Already in 1883, before any restoration was thought of, an anonymous donor had paid for a new reredos behind the altar to be erected. It is very Victorian in style and it would be interesting to know what it replaced.

In 1885 a guide book to the Norfolk Broads said that "the ancient parish church of St Catherine at Ludham is in a sad state of disrepair". The Rev. Henry Walker had been vicar for 30 years by then and perhaps it was the arrival of a new vicar, the Rev. John James Willmott in 1886 that caused people to realise that rather urgent repairs were needed.

In 1886 the parish magazine of Horsford and St Faiths, "Home Words", showed a drawing of childrens' seats in the old box pews in Ludham.

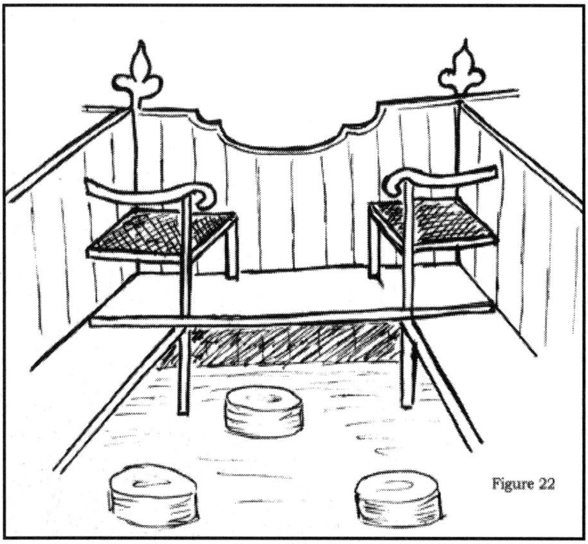

Figure 22

Over the next few years a vast restoration was under-taken. One wonders how the money was raised, for this was during a time when farming was in recession and many people were poor and disillusioned, even to the extent of emigrating... The repairs were all duly noted in one of the church registers and the Ludham Parish Magazine made comments from time to time.

By 1889 the first section of the restoration had been completed. The lead on the roofs had been recast and relaid. The weight of the old lead from three roofs before recasting was 27 tons and the new lead without the dross weighed 25½ tons. 27 hundredweights of lead at the west end of the nave was in better condition than the rest, so this was only rehammered.

The nave and aisle roof timbers were repaired; oak being substituted for the deal that had been used in earlier repairs. The south aisle was completely renewed in oak, exactly after the pattern of the old one with bosses and cresting. The north aisle roof was repaired.

Plate 72.

The Hammer Beam Roof of the Nave, with Alternate Long Wallposts and the Wheel of St. Catherine in Alternate Spandrels.

Photograph, the author.

The twelve clerestory windows had stonework repaired and were reglazed with lead. The south aisle gable wall and window were repaired; the stained glass Slipper memorial window would be placed there 31 years later in 1920.

On July 3 1890 the Vestry Meeting were shown plans for the future rearrangement of the church. These were accepted with no objections.

First the inside walls were scraped, then plastered above the sill line with Portland cement rendering beneath. In doing this, five recesses were found. The squint was unblocked and in it was found the clasped stone hand, which fitted neatly onto a socket on the south aisle wall, where it still is. This would have been originally for a sanctus bell rope, with the squint enabling the man who pulled the bell to see through to the high altar for the moment of the raising of the Host.

The pillars were repaired and cleaned and their red brick bases exposed. The rood stairs, where the B.A.A. had found the tympanum boards, were restored. They do not lead anywhere, for the rood loft across the chancel arch was destroyed in about 1550.

The old box pews and other seating were removed, the floor tiles and grave slabs taken up and six inches of soil removed. All open vaults and graves were filled in and then a ten inch layer of dry rubble and lime were put down before replacing the old tiles and the gravestones, new tiles being added where necessary. The font was removed to its present position and raised upon York stone steps. The emplacement of the pews was floored with two and a half-inch wood blocks.

New pews were installed, using four fronts and sixty benches. Cornish and Gaynor of North Walsham inserted old oak poppy-head bench ends onto the new pews wherever possible.

A temporary vestry (it is still there ....) was made from panels from the old pulpit.

Plate 73.

Photograph from old guide book showing side of vestry, (note beautiful linenfold panelling behind the chest), two pieces of old wooden tracery, the chest of c.1600 and a wooden lectern, which no longer exists.

The tympanum boards were recovered from the vicarage and were replaced in the chancel arch and the arms of Elizabeth I on canvas were hung behind on the chancel side of the arch.

Plate 74. The Arms of Queen Elizabeth I. Photograph, the author.

Originally, the rood screen, erected in 1493, would have supported the rood loft, with vaulting underneath. Access to this was from the stairway. Until the reign of Edward VI (1547-53) all churches had these with carvings of the Crucifixion (the rood) above. All were lost at this time when catholic symbols were destroyed or defaced, like St Jerome's Cardinal's hat and St. Gregory's papal crown on the screen below.

The painting of the Crucifixion on the boards of the tympanum is probably local work and is thought to have been painted during the time of the catholic Mary Tudor (1553-58) to replace in a hurry the rood destroyed in the previous reign. The canvas arms of Elizabeth I exactly fit the same shape and these were no doubt put up to cover the tympanum when Mary lost her head and her sister came to the throne and we were back to being protestant again and it was a prudent thing to do. Much later, all these were taken down and hidden in the staircase, perhaps during Cromwell's time, until they were found again in 1879.

During further restoration work in 1890 the inside of the tower was cleaned and repaired, the lower door to the stairs was mended and the first floor timbers were repaired, with a deal floor laid over and a moveable trap in the centre. New irons were fixed for the bell ropes.

The bells had already been rehung 64 years previously, back in 1826. One bell was then recast and all set in a new frame, and the clock altered, all at a cost of £80.11.0.

During 1890 the whole collection of thirteen monumental brasses was found in a box. These were replaced in their original positions. They include one of the oldest brasses in Norfolk, that of Thomas of Honing, sometime rector of Potter Heigham, who died in 1351. There are only five in Norfolk older than this one, which is in the south aisle.

By 1895 the old clock works were worn out and silent for several years, so some good secondhand works were obtained from Thwaites and Reed of Clerkenwell. The hands were lengthened to suit the old clock face, which was repainted.

After all this work, it was decided at a Vestry meeting (which by now had become the church council) in 1896 to insure the church with the Ecclesiastical Buildings Office for the sum of £2000. In the same year extensive repairs were made to the roof of the tower.

Two years later, the Ecclesiastical Commissioners, who because of the earlier connection with St Benets Abbey, are responsible for the upkeep of the chancel, repaired its outside walls and plastered the inside walls, and also deepened the drainage trench around the outside.

Just into the next century in 1902 both porches were restored, with the south turret stairs being rebuilt. At the same time eight standard lamps and a bracket lamp were given to the church. These were oil lamps, for the church did not have electricity until 1931.

Thus ended a Victorian restoration of a beautiful medieval church, that was carried out in very good taste throughout, under the guidance of the vicar from 1886 to 1908, the Rev. John J. Willmott.

Sources:
Register of Baptisms and Burials, 1808
Ludham Parish Magazines.
H.Munro Cautley, Norfolk Churches, 1949,
Norman Adlard & Co Ltd.
St Benets Abbey, Norfolk, Joan Snelling 1971,
revised W.F. Edwards 1983.

Plate 75. Old Postcard of the Church before 1920.

1894, Death of Sherwood William Page

Plate 76.

Sherwood Page was born in 1823 at Page's Farm, the eldest son of William Sherwood Page and his wife, Elizabeth, nee Ransome. After his marriage to Harriet Bately, the young couple lived at How Hill Farm and the two farms, being adjoining, were worked together. Harriet bore him three sons and died aged 35 in 1856. Sherwood then married her sister, Louisa Bately, but as this marriage was technically illegal, it took place in London.

After his death on 26 November 1894, the following obituary appeared in the Yarmouth Independent Newspaper on December 1st.

"Sherwood Page gone! It is hard to realise that his grand presence and cheery manner have passed beyond our ken. Not more than a month ago he came to our office (having for many years written our Agricultural Notes), and at that time, though he entered upon his 70th year, there was no sign of any decadence of that physical and intellectual force by which he has been able 'to make his merit known' as a public man, as well as an agriculturalist. He was then looking forward with eager interest and hope to the election and working of the District and Parish Councils Act under the new conditions and had for some time rendered excellent service in the Flegg Hundreds by his lucid explanatory lectures on the great legislative enactment that confers such vastly extended powers of local self government.

Mr Sherwood Page was the son of a farmer and a native of Ludham. Some years were spent in Holland in making himself aquainted with the peculiar skilful farming of that country. On returning to England he took land at Stokesby and afterwards at Ludham and Oby in succession, the farm he possessed up to the time of his death passing into his hands at the death of his father in 1876. Busy, thrifty and always on the alert, he turned to good account the knowledge he had gained among the careful and clever Dutch cultivators.

Politically he was a most consistent Liberal and did his best to further the principles in which he believed. When the County Council was about to take the place of the old purely magisterial rule he was elected to represent West Flegg; defeating in the contest the strongest possible clerical candidate of the district and at the election three years later he was returned unopposed. He regularly attended the meetings of the Council and exercised a very active part in the conduct of affairs.

As much can be said for his association with the East and West Flegg Incorporation; doing his utmost as a member of that body to serve both the ratepayers and the poor. But even those duties did not satisfy altogether his earnest wish to be 'up and doing for others'. For many years he most generously supported the Ragged School, Northgate Street, and he regularly came to Yarmouth every Sunday in shine and shower to address the children

As a Wesleyan he rendered constant and hearty service to the church. His annual gathering of the Easter Fair People for tea and counsel happened only once a year, but there can be no doubt that it was fruitful in good results. In these, and in other ways, Mr Sherwood Page used his talents and his means to make the world better than he found it. He was twice married and leaves a widow and three sons to whom we tender our deepest sympathy in their loss.

The funeral takes place on Friday afternoon at Ludham where Mr Page's father and other relatives are interred."

Among many, the following are recorded as being present at the funeral in Ludham:
Mrs Sherwood Page (nee Louisa Crow Bately); Charles Bately Page and John William Page, (sons); Mrs William Augustus Page, sister-in-law. Mrs George Durrant Preston and Mr G.D.F. Preston, niece. Mr Alfred Neave, Miss Knights and Miss Lown.

Fifteen years later, another funeral took place in Ludham churchyard when Sherwood Page's grandson, Charles Bately Page, aged 23 and Gregory Hazard Page, aged 37 (a son of Sherwood's brother, William Augustus and Hebe Page) were both drowned in a boating accident on the river.

Source:
Information and photograph kindly supplied by Raymond Page, from his History of the Page Family of Ludham and Oby in the County of Norfolk, The Senior Line, 1765 - 1983.
Deposited in the Local History Dept. Norfolk Studies Library.

Plate 77.

Election Time.

An early twentieth century election
Left to right:
Dennis Brookes
Alfred Goodwin
George Hayhurst
Colonel Worship
Ebeneezer Newton

The building on the left was Brook's Garage with petrol pump. In the centre distance, the little flint cottage, known as the Nook, now demolished, is just visible.

Provenance of Photograph unknown.

Plate 78. Womack Staithe, showing the malthouse, a wherry loading goods and Newtons' shed for storing coal. Old postcard.

1895, Election Riots and Emigration

In July 1895 there was a parliamentary election in the area and Rider Haggard was the Tory candidate and Robert Price was the Liberal. The Eastern Daily Press gave an account of election riots in Stalham and Ludham, and several indignant people wrote letters to the paper, of which the following are a few extracts:

"First Mr Price and his party were pelted with rotten eggs by a mob on Martham Green. This was followed by disgraceful scenes at Ludham and Stalham. About 500 people gathered in Stalham to see the candidates and some were noisy and riotous through drink. Here Mr Haggard and his party were attacked and forced to take refuge in the Swan Inn. It is not quite clear what happened at Ludham, but it was obviously a similar scene."

"When the telegram was received announcing the coming of the police, these pot-valiant boozers immediately vanished from the scene." "Drink, and drink alone, was the cause of these disgraceful scenes". "The Ludham Roughs" from Doubly Disgusted. "Disgraceful scenes at Ludham was the dirty work of a number of drunken fools. Perhaps Mr Haggard's rough treatment at Ludham was the result of Mr Price's party getting disgusting treatment at Martham the previous Wednesday, when rotten eggs were thrown at a Stalham Liberal!"

"Some 500 people congregated in Stalham to see the candidates pass through, a few noisy and riotous through drink. Mr Rider Haggard's outrider rode in Stalham with a formidable hunting whip in his hand and gave those who hindered his progress a nasty blow on the head. Many of us thought it was indiscreet on his part. Mr Rider Haggard was in the Swan Inn".

All correspondents seemed agreed on one thing; "We boldly aver that drink, and drink alone, was the cause" and another. "We appeal to both parties in Stalham and Ludham to lay aside all bitterness of party strife and join in one common attack upon the one enemy of peace and progress - the strong drink".

Mr Robert Price finally won the election, later to become Sir Robert Price.

It was not surprising that there were riots, as men were getting desperate. Agriculture was in a deep depression. In the 1870s several years of appalling weather had ruined harvests. Wheat, which had sold at 55 shillings per quarter in 1870-4 was down to 28 shillings in 1895. Corn growers faced ruin as imported corn flooded in from the U.S.A., Canada and the Argentine, and these countries quadrupled their export of grain to Britain between 1870 and 1900. East Anglia suffered the most and there were dilapidated farms and bankruptcies with the inevitable result that all those dependant on the farmers' prosperity suffered too.

In Ludham some men decided to emigrate. There was an emigration agent in the village; Robert Newton, born in 1829, a carpenter by trade and son of the publican and postmaster at the Rose and Crown. In 1890 he was the branch secretary of the National Agricultural Labourers' Union for both Ludham and Horning. In March 1888 five people left for Canada and the U.S.A., but there were many more over the years. Newton's son was still helping men to emigrate at the turn of the century. I have two letters written in 1973 from Robert Watson who emigrated to America in 1923 with over a hundred other young men from Ludham and nearby villages. These movements show in the population figures with a loss of 342 people between 1851 and 1901.

Source:
Eastern Daily Press, July 1895.
Note, Arthur Newton, born 1886, told me that his grandparents actually came from the U.S.A. to live in Ludham. This was the same family as Robert Newton, the emigration agent.

A Look at the Parish in 1900

Britain entered the twentieth century in the grip of war, just as she had done in 1800. Then it was against Napoleon, this time it was the Boer war in South Africa, but it was not to last much longer.

While recruiting for the army for this war, it was noticed that many men were physically poor specimens and under-fed. Rural living standards had been slow to improve and farm workers were among the lowest paid of all workers with an income only a little over half the average wage.

The population in Ludham had dropped to its lowest level; in 1801 it had been 724 and in 1901 it was down to 639. Thus 342 people had left the parish in the fifty years since the mid-century peak of 981.

The building of the Board School in 1873 and the arrival of compulsory education had slowly widened the horizons of the village people and influenced their hopes and ambitions. Also the coming of the railway to nearby Potter Heigham in the 1880s was a liberation. With increasing education and access to a wider world many Ludham men and women became dissatisfied with agricultural unemployment, poor rural housing and only the prospect of the Smallburgh workhouse in their old age. Many migrated to the towns, where the higher industrial wages were an attraction. Many also sought the help of Robert Newton, the emigration agent, and went further still, to Canada and the U.S.A.

The farms themselves had changed. Arable farming was no longer profitable. The price of wheat was very low and cheaper imported corn had quadrupled from overseas. At the census of fifty years before there had been twenty-one farmers; in 1900 Kelly's directory gives only ten, most of whom were tenant farmers, as the land of almost all the parish was owned by six absentee landlords. Comparing the map (Figure 23) showing these men with the map of farmland in 1800 (Figure 1), one is struck by the fact that their holdings of land are almost exactly the same as the extents of the old open fields.

LUDHAM PARISH

Figure 23 SHOWING THE BIG LANDOWNERS IN 1900

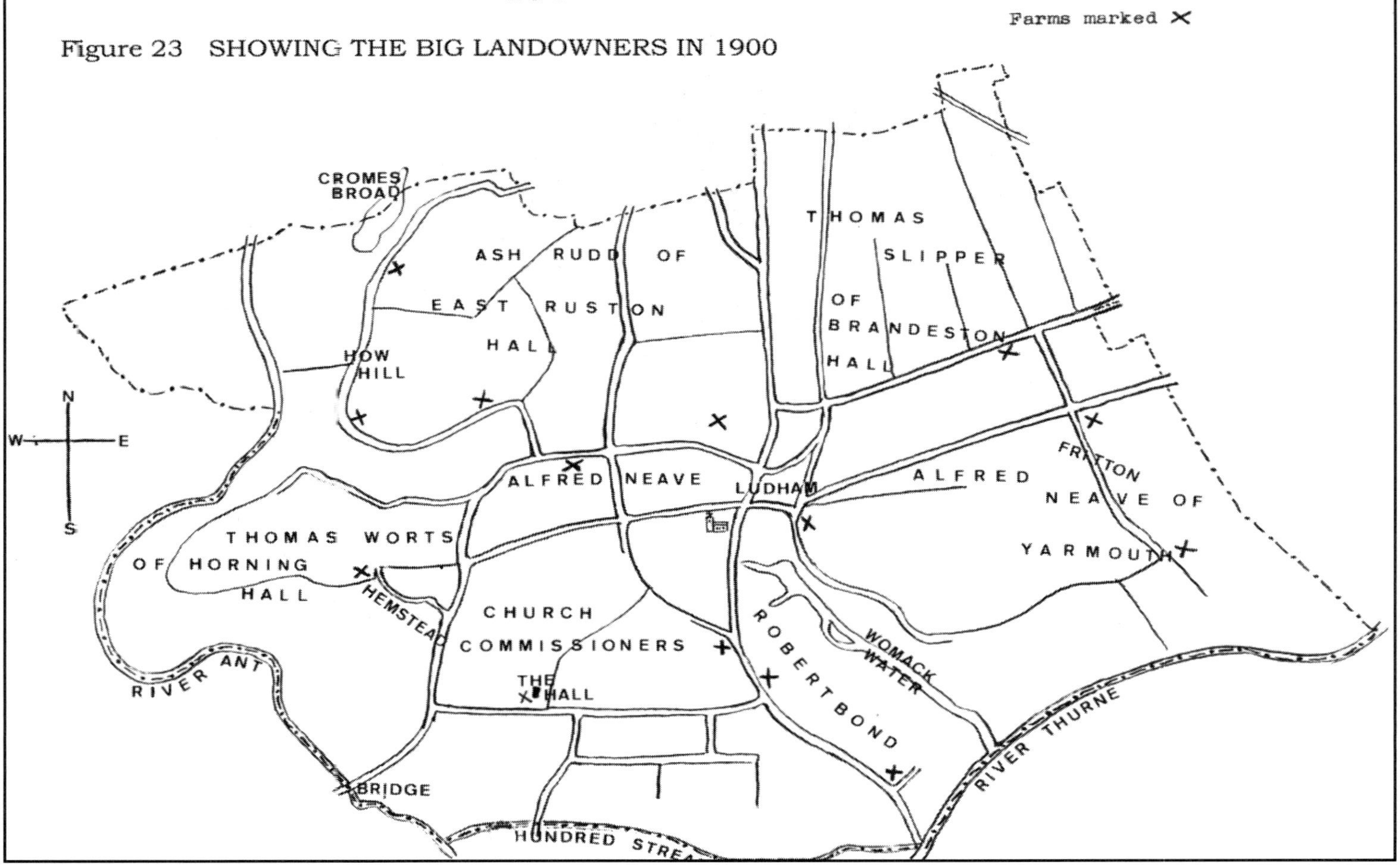

Thomas Slipper of Brandeston Hall, whose family had previously lived and farmed at Fritton Farm, owned all the north-east of the parish and farmed it with a bailiff, James Beevor. This area was once Ludham Field. Ash Rudd of East Ruston Hall owned a large part of the north-west, which had once been How Field. Alfred Neave, who lived in Yarmouth, owned four farms, three of which formed the old open field of Bears Hirn; Beeches Farm, Green Farm and High House Farm. He also owned Laurels Farm in the centre of the parish. The smaller Clint Field was farmed by Thomas Worts of Horning Hall with his bailiff, Richard Gibbs. The Ecclesiastical Commissioners still owned the Ludham Hall estate and the Goose Croft lands were owned by Robert Bond of Norwich, and included Manor Farm, Coldharbour and Hall Common Farm, where his family had lived.

In the village in 1900 there were still numerous trades and industries, in spite of the depression. There were three blacksmiths, for the horse was still the chief means of transport. The millwrights, Englands, were still flourishing; Edwin England was landlord of the Kings Arms after the death of his father, Daniel, as well as being an engineer and a manufacturer of pumps. John Davey retailed beer at the Bakers Arms, with the bakehouse ovens at the rear continuing to cook the bread and pies and sometimes meat, of those who had only an open hearth at home.

The house on Staithe Road, once the vicarage, then the Spread Eagle public house, had by 1900 become a temperance hotel, whose landlord, Robert Ward, also managed to be a grocer, baker, ironmonger and draper... No doubt he used the little bakehouse next door, for this remained in use for quite a few more years. Arthur Newton remembered delicious hot cross buns there...

The widowed Harriot England still had her grocer's shop at the north end of the Street and Clarissa Fairhead - now 84 - was still in her small shop on Stocks Hill, next to Grace Lyon's larger general store. Arthur Newton remembered Miss Fairhead as a very deaf old lady, on whom he and other small boys used to play tricks to distract her. He also recalled that Tom Thurgate the carrier kept his four-wheeled cart in a shed near the vicarage drive. Helen Thurgate was postwoman at the post office in the thatched row on the Norwich Road.

By the end of the nineteenth century the Broads were becoming very popular for recreational sailing and yachts would often be moored at Womack. Arthur Newton, when a very small boy, used to sing this song to visiting yachtsmen for pennies;

"Hi John Barleycorn, Hi John Barleycorn,
Young and old, we praise thy soul,
Hi John Barleycorn"

Presumably this little ditty was in praise of barley for beer! He also recollected two regattas on Womack, which had then a much larger area of open water.

Clifford Kittle's memories of Womack concern Ted Griffen, the eel catcher, who lived in a boat on Womack. He and other boys used to bung up the boats' chimney, and then run before the smoke drove out the irate eel catcher...

Plate 79. Clifford Kittle said that this photograph was of Ted Griffen on his boat. The chimney is certainly accessible from the bank. Old postcard.

The house at How Hill was built in 1904 by Edward Boardman. Clifford Kittle, whose father farmed at How Hill, remembered the bricks for the house being carted from Potter Heigham station in waggons pulled by traction engines. These were so heavy that one went through the road surface onto sand.

Amongst the memories of Arthur Newton, Clifford Kittle and others, one subject was mentioned continually; the loss of the Old Staithe for public use. They all said that, about 1906, Dr James Gordon, who lived at the Manor, bribed Sam Hicks, owner of the wherry, Early Bird, (see Plate 60) to say that the staithe was private and that he paid to moor and unload his wherry there. Fencing was erected across the end of the staithe, but this was soon pulled up by angry villagers, some of whom ended up at North Walsham police court. Whatever happened, the staithe was lost to public use and only the name of the road remains to remind us of it; Staithe Road with no staithe...

In 1900 Ludham still had its medieval bridge, but it was not to last much longer. Clifford Kittle said that it was built upon oak trees, laid "arse to head", and that when it was tried to put water pipes across in 1912, the oaks were cut off as they impeded the pipes. This upset the balance and the bridge began to tilt, so it was demolished and rebuilt in 1914. (see Plates 4 and 8.)

The actual landscape of Ludham parish did not change during the nineteenth century, apart from the planting of hedges in the early years. It still has not changed, as we look at it nearly another hundred years later, apart from the removal of some of those hedges and the loss of a few fine buildings.

It is still a green and pleasant land.

Sources:
Kelly's directory, 1900.
The memories of Arthur Newton and Clifford Kittle.
I am grateful to Mark Goodwin for the names of the six landowners in 1900 from his 1975 school work on Ludham.

Plate 80. Ludham Football Team, 1905. Left to right, standing; Albert England, Arthur Newton, Jack Thrower, Charles Clarke, Fred Riches, Tom Thrower, William Fitzhugh, Bob Tillett. Sitting; Fred Burton, Jack Tillet, Sydney Grapes, George Hayhurst, William England.

te 81. *Ludham Village from the West, 1966. Photograph, the author.*

BIBLIOGRAPHY

HUGH BRAUN, Old English Houses, 1962, Faber.

GEORGE EWART EVANS, The Horse in the Furrow, 1960, Faber & Faber.

KELLY, directories, 1883, 1900

ROBERT MALSTER, Wherries and Waterways, 1971, Terence Dalton Ltd.

H. MUNRO CAUTLEY, Norfolk Churches, 1949, Norman Adlard & Co.

HOWARD NEWBY, Country Life, A Social History of Rural England, 1987, Penguin.

RAYMOND PAGE, History of the Page Family 1765-1983, Norfolk Studies Library

MICHAEL E. ROSE, The English Poor Law, 1971, David & Charles.

ARTHUR C.SMITH, Drainage Windmills of the Norfolk Marshes, 1978, Stevenage Museum Publications.

JOAN M. SNELLING, St Benets Abbey, Norfolk, 1971, Revised W.F.EDWARDS, 1983, St Benets Committee, Diocesan Offices, Norwich.

W.E.TATE, The Parish Chest, 1960, Cambridge University Press

W.E.TATE, The English Village Community and the Enclosure Movement, 1967 Victor Gollancz.

REX WAILES, The English Windmill, 1954, Routledge & Keegan Paul.

REX WAILES, Norfolk Windmills, part II, 1955-57, Newcomen Society Transactions, Vol: 30.

WHITES Norfolk Directory, 1845, David & Charles reprint, 1969.

ARTHUR YOUNG, General View of the Agriculture of the County of Norfolk, 1804, David & Charles reprint, 1969.

AN HISTORICAL ATLAS OF NORFOLK 1993, Norfolk Museums Service.